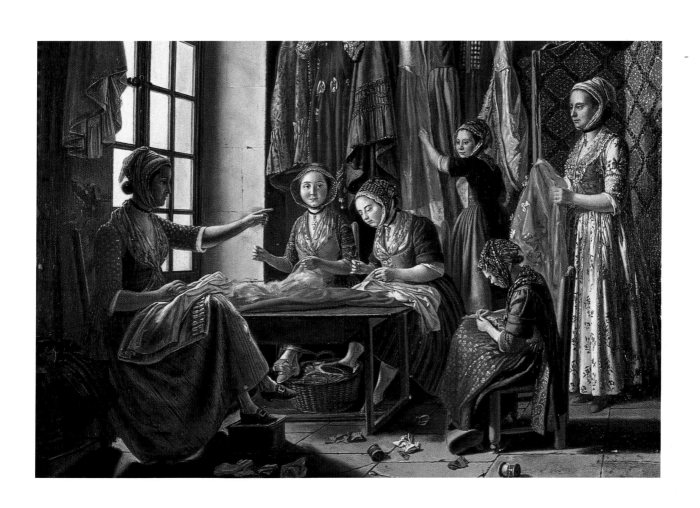

QUILTS *of* PROVENCE

~ *Kathryn Berenson* ~

The Art and Craft of French Quiltmaking

FOREWORD BY MICHEL BIEHN

POTTER
CRAFT

New York

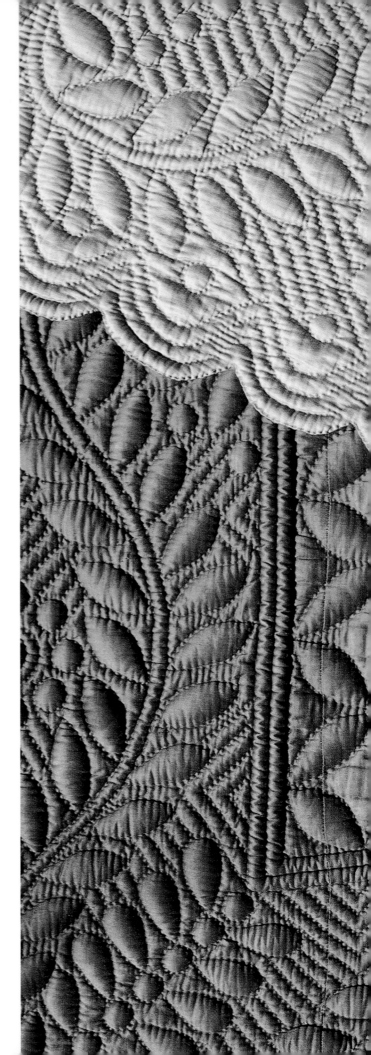

Published in the United States by Potter Craft,
an imprint of the Crown Publishing Group,
a division of Random House, Inc., New York
www.crownpublishing.com
www.pottercraft.com

Potter Craft and *Clarkson N. Potter* are trademarks, and *Potter*
and colophon are registered trademarks of Random House, Inc.

Library of Congress Cataloging-in-Publication Data

Berenson, Kathryn.
Quilts of Provence: the art and craft of French quiltmaking /
Kathryn Berenson; foreword by Michel Biehn. — Rev. ed.
p.   cm.
Original ed. published: New York : Henry Holt, 1996.
"An Archetype Press Book."
Includes bibliographical references and index.
ISBN 978-0-307-34552-3 (hardcover with jacket: alk. paper)
1. Quilts—France—Provence. I. Title.
NK9149.A3P763 2008
746.460944´9—dc22
2006037422

ISBN 978-0-307-34552-3

Produced by Archetype Press, Inc.
Project Director: Diane Maddex
Editor: Gretchen Smith Mui
Editorial Assistant: Kristi Flis
Designer: Robert L. Wiser

Printed in China

1   3   5   7   9   10   8   6   4   2

Page 1: *"L'Atelier d'une Couturière à Arles"* (circa 1760),
Antoine Raspal.
Page 2: *Eighteenth-century bedcovers of colorfully dyed bourrettes,
made from the rough outer strands of silkworm cocoons.*
Page 3: *Engraving of Marseilles (1841).*
Pages 4–5: *Nineteenth-century quilted Provençal bedcovers.*
Pages 8–9: *"L'entrée du port de Marseille" (1754), Joseph Vernet.*

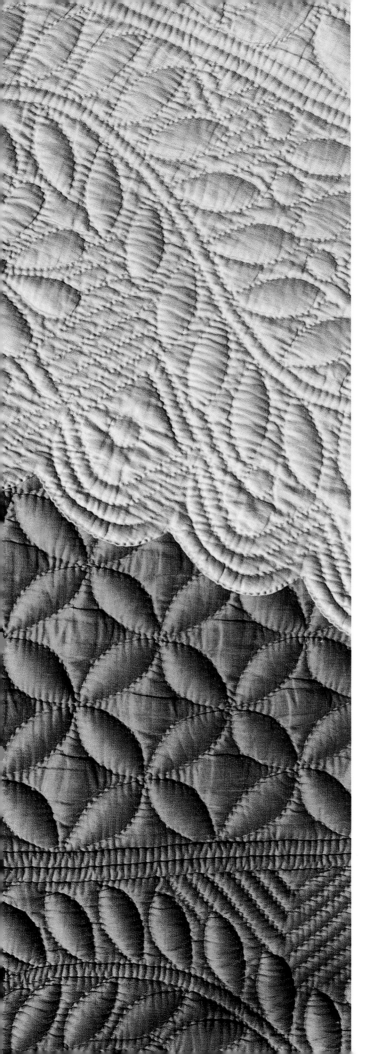

Contents

Foreword

I discovered antique textiles about fifteen years ago. I knew nothing about them then but bought on instinct, seduced by their intense colors, their beautiful decoration, their attractive forms. They accumulated in my little shop in Aix-en-Provence—cashmere shawls, a courtesan's gown, a piano cover, piles of Provençal bedcovers—all manner of textiles in ravishing colors, prints, and textures. I could not have said if they were silk or cotton, and I was absolutely ignorant about their origins, their dates, and the techniques that brought them into being.

I came to buy a lot of pretty women's clothing, several Provençal *caracos,* neck scarves, and numerous quilted *jupons.* Enchanted with their bright colors and the gaiety of their prints—small floral sprays punctuated with birds and monkeys, temples, and fountains—I put them on mannequins in my shop window. As I dressed the window I was a little nervous and asked myself how I could be so naive as to think that someone would buy these garments, so unwearable despite their charms. Just then an elegant lady, clad in a long fur coat and holding three handsome Cavaliers–King Charles on a leash, pushed open the door to my shop. In a strong American accent she demanded the price of my pretty costumes. "I will take them all," she quickly added. "But you do not seem to know much about them. Would you like me to tell you what they are?"

From that day Lillian Williams and I began a rich friendship. She opened the doors of her fantastic collection to me and taught me what I know today about the fabrics and costumes of eighteenth-century France. She knew this period better than anyone—all that the French did in their daily life two centuries ago, their customs and values, their work and play, their fashions and toilette, even their makeup. I have always been amused and astonished by American awareness of the French art of living—the essential elements of our culture.

How marvelous that another American, Kathryn Berenson, offers us this book on the history and techniques of Provence's quilted needlework tradition, one as serious as it is passionate and as well documented as it is elegant. This story of the art of corded and stuffed quilted work—an art that long ago left China, crossed India and Persia, came to southern Europe, and eventually conquered the New World, influencing the development of the magnificent art of American quilts—finally gives Provence its rightful place in history.

Kathryn Berenson tells us how this passage from east to west stopped for a time in Provence, where, pushed by a wind charged with the pollens of another world, the techniques of quilting flourished from the seventeenth century on, first in Marseilles and then through all of Provence. She shows how large commercial efforts brought about the exportation of these finely stitched works, allowing them to continue on their way to propagate others with their delicate savoir faire.

Thank you, Kathryn.

Michel Biehn, l'Isle-sur-la-Sorgue

"PORTRAIT DE JEUNE FILLE EN COSTUME D'ARLES" (1779) by Antoine Raspal helps document dates of needlework styles. This Arlesienne put on her best for her portrait—a ramoneur-printed cotton jacket artfully cut to show off her white cotton camisole, its neckline and sleeves bordered with broderie de Marseille.

Introduction

A CORDED EIGHTEENTH-CENTURY BRODERIE DE MARSEILLE BEDCOVER *measures more than one hundred inches on each side, yet every square inch is filled with miniature flowers. From a large vase in the center, enclosed in an eight-point medallion, flowers meander along the sides and corners, the intertwined floral forms completely filling the ground. The pattern channels were worked in a running stitch at about twenty-two stitches per inch.*

"Is it any better in Heaven, my friend Ford,
Than you found it in Provence?"

William Carlos Williams, "To Ford Madox Ford in Heaven" (1939)

HE STRONG GOLDEN SUNLIGHT *of Provence illuminates all detail. Each leaf, each flower petal, the small curve of a snail shell, the refined form of carved architectural stone, everything that curves and swells, everything that recedes into shadow—all are limned with light. The same intensity of light illuminates colors in every hue, from subtle gray-green olive leaves and pale blue lavender florets to red-burnished pomegranates and golden sunflower petals. This is, after all, the land that enchanted the painters Paul Cézanne, Vincent Van Gogh, Henri Matisse, and Marc Chagall.* ❧ *Perhaps it is this quality of light that influenced Provence's needlework tradition, a technique dependent on the play of light and shadow to reveal a decorative pattern stitched in three dimensions. Nestled among the many charms of this pleasant part of the world, in southeastern France bordering the Mediterranean*

THE SOFT HUE OF FLOWERING THYME *(above) is mirrored in a Provençal silk quilt (opposite) made about 1830, during the reign of Charles X. The material combined with traditional Provençal quilting motifs—melons, kashmir cones, pomegranates, and flowers—evokes a sense of prosperity.*

12

A PALETTE OF PROVENÇAL COLORS: Olive trees stand over a field
of full-flowering lavender near Grasse (below left). Throughout the centuries
Provençal's signature sunflowers have provided artistic inspiration (below right).

Sea, is a distinctly Provençal heritage of splendid quilted works—bedcovers, clothing, and small decorative accessories of great beauty and needle skills. Long before the birth of France, when Provence was its own kingdom, accomplished craftswomen of the region took common needles, thread, and textiles and launched a remarkable tradition that resulted in quilted articles both useful and extraordinarily lovely.

Provence was a fertile setting for the development of cultural arts. Since the seafaring Greeks settled there in 600 B.C., Provence has attracted people of diverse cultures, power, and means—adventurers, soldiers, traders, merchants, and emissaries. Julius Caesar conquered it on his way to Britain in 51 B.C.

The Holy Roman Empire loosely annexed it in A.D. 1032. Crusaders and pilgrims from all over Europe passed through Provence en route to their holy wars and destinations. Popes held exiled court in Avignon throughout most of the fourteenth century—from 1306 to 1403—when Rome was mired in political strife. In the fifteenth century, from 1434 to 1480, René of Anjou ruled his extensive kingdom from Aix-en-Provence. Provence was separate from France until René's death and for centuries afterward acted with an independence irritating to its French rulers.

Provence's Mediterranean city of Marseilles was a natural, protected port that from prehistory served as an *entrepôt* for trade in luxurious consumer goods

The deep yellows, oranges, and reds of spices reverberate throughout a Provençal market (below left). A low stone wall hung with red poppies encloses an orchard (below right).

arriving in ships by bale, basket, bundle, and cask. Spices, sweet figs, oils, and unguents from Alexandria, Cairo, Tunisia, and Aleppo; finely woven, richly dyed, and embroidered silk goods from Sicily; fine cottons from Cairo—all of these goods and more came to Marseilles. As early as the thirteenth century domestic goods traveled overland: rough silks produced in the Cévennes region to be shipped to Tunis, rough woven cloth from Avignon, and striped goods from Paris destined for the Arabian peninsula.

The geography of Provence, with its low mountains, fertile valleys, and rocky cliffs overlooking the Mediterranean, has always been inviting to human habitation. Its temperate climate and plentiful water sources—springs, streams, and rivers—cause lavender, rosemary, thyme, grapevines, almond and olive trees, and orchards and gardens to flourish.

All of these elements—cultural, commercial, and geographical—played a part in the development of the exquisite needle arts of Provence. The lavish courts of popes and kings celebrated this work and inspired domestic industries to develop new textile products to titillate regal tastes. Luxury cloth from foreign markets served first as inspiration and later as the material for locally created needle art works. Mediterranean shipping routes encouraged importation and exportation of goods. The bounty of the land allowed Provençals time to explore needle crafts.

Plentiful harvests of fields, gardens, and orchards even provided inspiration to needlewomen who transferred the shapes of flowers, grapes and grapevines, herbs, and melons to decorative corded, stuffed, and quilted designs on clothing and bedcovers.

French Confections

In ordinary quilting a filling element, such as batting or cording, is sandwiched between two textile layers, all of which are held together with lines of stitching. Quilting is an old invention; various forms of quilted articles have been dated to prehistory on several continents. Quilted articles were functional; they insulated the human body from cold and protected it from hard blows (quilted armor was especially useful before the invention of the arrow). The dimpled pattern on the surface of a quilted article, created by stitching lines that held together the layers, was secondary to function.

What distinguished the work of Provençal needle-women was their vision of the decorative possibilities inherent in these lines of stitching. They developed the ability to realize complex, minutely detailed patterns in beautiful, well-proportioned motifs merely through the play of light and shadow on the surface of a textile.

The Provençal craft of quilting began with simple

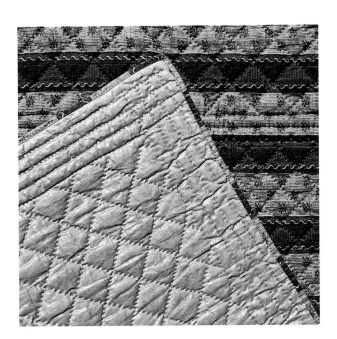 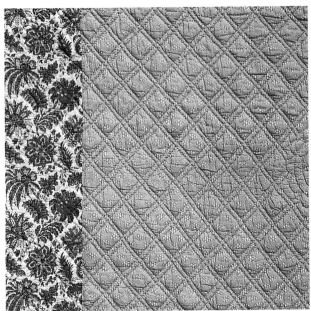

PROVENÇAL COLORS REFLECTED IN PROVENÇAL QUILTS:
A black-and-violet silk vanne (a small, decorative bedcover) (above left) and a gold
cotton fenêtre quilt bordered with an indienne (above right) display Provençal colors.

forms—for example, lines stitched in a grid pattern through thick bedcovers. The craft developed over centuries into delicately stuffed and corded, stylized floral forms that graced articles of dress and interior domestic decor. Three hundred years ago thousands of professional needlewomen worked in Marseilles ateliers to produce these exquisite articles, made for export throughout Europe and to the Americas. When the export business declined, the women of Provence continued to make quilted pieces for their own use, still stitched in decorative high relief. Knowledgeable French call these elegant works "confections" and refer to the process of stitching them as "embroidery from within."

Provençal Needlework Terms

Throughout this book readers will note the use of the term "needlewomen" to denote those who produced the famed Provençal needlework. Although it is conceivable that some men were employed in the needlework ateliers of Marseilles, Arles, Avignon, and other Provençal cities during the seventeenth and eighteenth centuries, historic documents refer only to women workers, if gender is noted at all. (The proprietors of these ateliers, as indicated in historic documents, are without exception men. No available records reveal the gender of or any other information about the designers

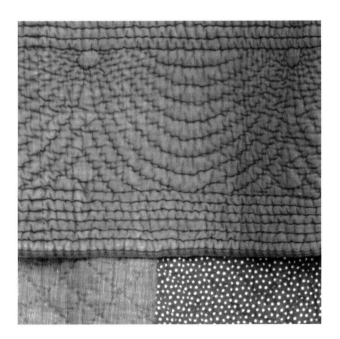 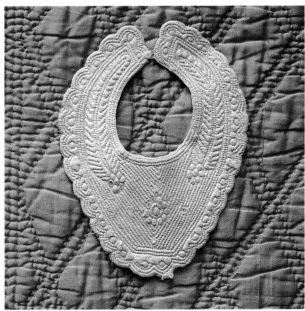

A quilt made of cotton dyed as blue as the Provençal sky (above left) is quilted in drapery swag motifs. A corded broderie de Marseille bib from the nineteenth century (above right) features rosemary branches, flowers, and a scalloped edge.

of these quilted articles.) Domestically produced quilted pieces were considered "women's work," although some quilted articles probably came from the hands of skilled men. In adopting the term "needlewomen," the author has decided to err on the side of the majority.

The adjective "Marseilles" applied to a textile object in England and the United States generally refers to an all-white cotton article with a raised, textured pattern, always whole cloth (one type of fabric or weave). The Provençal quilting tradition, however, included colored and printed cottons and plain colored and multicolored woven silks. In the last two hundred years the adjective "Marseilles" has been applied without clear distinction to a number of textile categories, particularly after the 1763 advent of loom-woven "Marseilles cloth." Museum curators have used the term "Marseilles quilt" to refer both to a handstitched corded, stuffed, and quilted bedcover and to a loom-woven bedcover, both produced within twenty-five years of each other yet neither made in Marseilles. Free-form spelling in old English and American inventories and advertisements, in which "Marseilles" became variously "Marcella," "marsella," "marcels," "Marseils," "Marsala," or "Marsyle," exacerbates the confusion. Even now terminology is perplexing. Many mail-order catalogues offer machine-woven bedspreads under the name "matelassé," but in French the word *matelassé* refers to a hand-quilted textile.

SOPHISTICATED QUILTING PATTERNS enhance this Provençal bedcover, made about 1840. Drapery swags with a four-petaled flower in each corner make up the border, while a medallion appears in the center.

TWO TEXTILES LOOSELY TERMED "MARSEILLES CLOTH" (opposite) have similar designs
but were made by different methods. The piece on the top, with its puffed grid and parallel
diagonal lines, was stitched by hand in the early nineteenth century. The piece on the
bottom was woven on a machine-driven loom in the late nineteenth century.

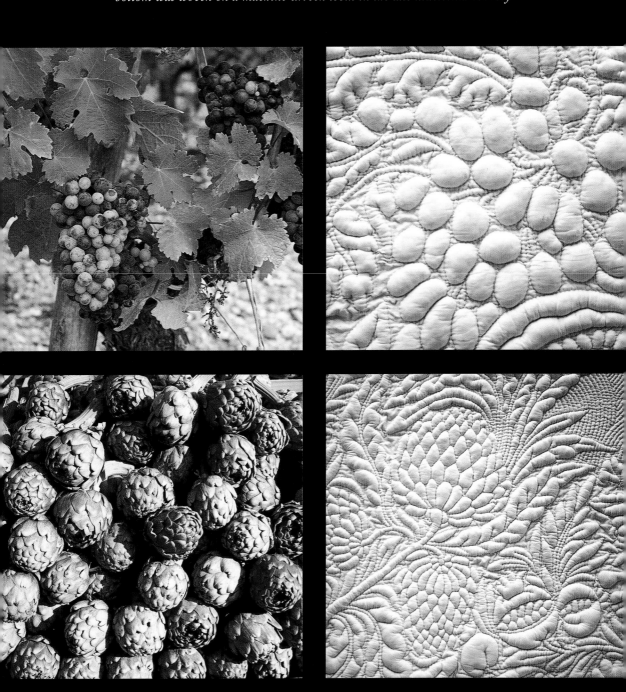

GRAPE AND ARTICHOKE MOTIFS (above), part of Provence's bounty,
were frequently worked into all-white broderie de Marseille quilts
of the late eighteenth and early nineteenth centuries.

The term "Italian quilting" has generally been used to refer to corded needlework. Although corded needlework was produced in ateliers in Sicily and Naples, the large amount of it produced elsewhere, particularly in Provence, belies the geographic association evoked by this term.

Finally, the spelling of the name of Provence's port city itself also requires some clarification. In English it is spelled with a final "s" ("Marseilles"). In French, however, it is spelled without the final consonant ("Marseille")—hence, the term *broderie de Marseille*.

French reference to Marseilles as the origin of fine quilted work apparently first appears in the duke of Luynes's 1750 inventory of the queen's bedroom at Fontainebleau outside Paris. Presumably, before that date everyone knew where this distinct quilted work originated. In this book references to quilted articles produced in Marseilles are identified by specific French terms—*broderie de Marseille* and *toiles piquées*—to reinforce their Provençal origins and distinguish them from English and American adaptations.

The finely quilted decorative needle art that came from the hands of professional and domestic needlewomen in Provence deserves the respect of its own terminology. As knowledge of the history and dispersion of this glorious work increases, it may change conventional thought about the origins of and influences on quilting traditions in Europe and the United States.

THIS HONEY-COLORED COTTON BEDCOVER, circa 1850, is quilted in a rounded diamond grid surrounded by a series of borders: parallel lines, almond shapes, and an undulating swag of leaves ending in a flower at the corner.

The Needle Arts of Provence

QUILTS STACKED UNDER A MURAL *of the port of Marseilles*
in the city's Villa Provençale capture the essence of the Provençal quilting tradition—
vibrant colors and robust, high-relief quilting.

PPRECIATION FOR QUALITY TEXTILES *in Provence reaches back to the origins of Provençal culture. A third-century Roman mosaic unearthed near the old port of Marseilles and exhibited at the Musée des Docks Romains illustrates this esteem. The mosaic shows a female bather in the midst of disrobing, her white garment falling in folds around her. Through the use of light and dark stone the robe is portrayed as artfully and meticulously as the comely bather herself.* ☙ *Since the arrival of Phocaeans from Greece who founded "Massalia" about 600 B.C., Marseilles has served as an important seaport and trading post. Archaeological excavations reveal that Marseilles, at various times under Greek, Roman, and independent rule, was continually involved in maritime trade across and beyond the Mediterranean and served as the trade center for inland commerce as well. Thus well positioned, Marseilles merchants could traffic in a wide range of*

A FRENCH COFFRET *(opposite) opens to divulge jewel-toned quilts stitched in sculptural forms—hallmarks of nineteenth-century Provençal needlework.* A FUCHSIA-COLORED SILK BOURRETTE *(above), bordered with strips from a red Provençal scarf print, forms the top of an eighteenth-century bedcover, quilted in a simple, double-line lozenge pattern.*

*AN EARLY MAP OF PROVENCE (opposite top) shows that Marseilles was
ideally situated for trade. Commerce with the continent followed the Rhone River,
while the rest of the world was accessible across the Mediterranean Sea.*

commercial products, including textiles, one of the most desirable. Louis Blancard in *Documents inédits sur le commerce de Marseille au moyen âge* cites records of this exchange: in 1218 a load of cotton from India left Marseilles for Tangier on board the *Bonaventure,* and in 1234 the ship owned by Creissesben and Company sailed from Marseilles to Tunis laden with silk from Provence. Marseilles agents received many qualities and weaves of cottons from India and fabulous silk textiles routed over land and sea from China and, later, in the fifteenth century, from Italy. Provence itself produced many fabrics woven from linen and hemp; in addition, rough silks produced north of Provence were shipped to Mediterranean markets through Marseilles.

Given such plentiful access to textiles, a ready supply of labor, and interested markets, Marseilles entrepreneurs naturally and successfully pursued production of textiles and finished textile articles for more than domestic consumption. According to Louis Chabaud in *Marseille et ses industries,* in the sixth century the pope commanded prelates in Marseilles and Arles to pay their annual tribute in ready-made clothing, not silver, so that he could dress his entourage in Rome. Twelfth-century crusaders passing through Marseilles spread the fame of the fine cotton *linge du corps* (garments worn under heavy outerwear), which were made for sale in the port city. Soft, absorbent cotton was considerably more comfortable than linen, wool, or hemp cloth under armor. In 1272 members of the Grand Council of

Venice so highly regarded Marseilles-made sail canvas that they granted it tax-free entry, notes Chabaud.

Quilted garments and other articles probably were among the trade goods handled in this active port. Quilted needlework originated thousands of years ago in Asia. Presumably it was transported to India and then to Europe, arriving through gateways such as Marseilles. Given its rich history in textile trade and production, Marseilles was likely one of the first European sites to appropriate this method of manipulating cloth and filling for practical and decorative uses. One of the earliest written references to quilted work in Provence appears in a 1297 inventory that credits the estate of the Marseilles ship captain Guillaume Ferrenc with two woolen pallets, one feather pillow, and one *courtepointe* (quilted bedcover), according to Gustave Arnaud d'Agnel's *Inventaires mobiliers du XIIIème siècle.* Many similar listings provide evidence that quilted bedcovers were widely used then and through the following century. Records do not indicate whether these quilted pieces were imported or produced locally. Not until the fifteenth century is there evidence of a cottage industry in Marseilles, where women in their *"petits ateliers à domicile"* created articles of quilted clothing for sale, the padded stitching making garments "warmer and more shapely in form," according to Gaston Rambert's *Histoire du commerce de Marseille.* Because these records are not detailed and so few textiles have survived, it is impossible to know what these pieces looked like or which textiles and quilting patterns were used.

*THE ANNUAL FAIR OF BEAUCAIRE in Provence (opposite bottom) was the general
clearinghouse for commerce — textiles and other eagerly sought goods — from all of Europe
from the fourteenth through the nineteenth centuries. Opening each year on July 21 and
lasting for eight days, it welcomed three hundred thousand visitors in times of peace.*

Aristocratic Origins

The first description of quilting motifs comes from a 1426 estate inventory of the countess of Avelin in the Château des Baux, near Arles in Provence, which lists bedcovers with motifs illustrating the stories of Alexander and Solomon. The figures were worked all in white "in the style of Naples," according to L. Barthélemy in the *Inventaire du château des Baux en 1426*. The passing reference to Italian work establishes a connection with another, well-known Italian textile—the "Story of Tristram" bedcover, an all-white corded, stuffed, and quilted bedcover illustrating in fourteen panels the story of Tristram from Arthurian legend. It is attributed to a needlework atelier in Sicily about 1395. Jonathan Holstein in "Sister Quilts from Sicily: A Pair of Renaissance Bedcovers" discusses what is either the other half of the Tristram piece or a matching work also depicting the Tristram story, attributed to the same Sicilian atelier. Yet a fourth piece is a quilted bedcover *"poincte de hommes et damoiselles [sic]"* (stitched with figures of men and women) identified in the bedchamber of King René of Anjou eight years after his death. It was listed in the 1488 inventory of the Bastide de Perignane near Aix-en-Provence, according to d'Agnel in *L'ameublement Provençal et Comtadin durant le*

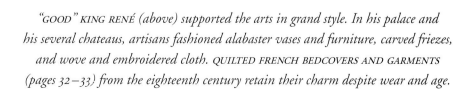

moyen âge et la Renaissance. These four all-white bedcovers use quilted needlework to depict human figures and have been attributed to Naples, Sicily, and Provence. Since 1266 all three regions had been ruled by the same political authority, the House of Anjou.

One key person reinforces the relationship among these four figurative pieces—"Good" King René of Anjou (1409–80), who ruled over this combined kingdom from his court in Aix-en-Provence. Beloved of his subjects, author of the *Book of Love*, composer of music and poetry, he was an avid patron of the arts. René made three voyages to Naples and Sicily, always returning with shiploads of luxury goods. He is also linked to a potential fifth all-white figurative bedcover. Marie-José Beaumelle in *Les arts décoratifs en Provence* credits, without documentation, René's wife, Jeanne de Laval, with stitching a corded, stuffed illustration of the story of Alexander, similar in style to the Tristram work and drawn from the same source.

These bedcovers were actually needlework texts— picture stories worked in sculptural relief using textiles, cording, and batting. This storytelling handwork tradition was apparently shared among artisans of Sicily, Naples, and Provence, whose cultural as well as political ties were made convenient by short, well-traveled shipping routes. René's interest in these luxury goods helped promote the mixing of these needle arts.

Commerce in Luxury Textiles

Marseilles entrepreneurs were known to adapt foreign needlework techniques to local advantage. According to Rambert's *Histoire du commerce de Marseille,* Marseilles agents recruited Italian embroiderers to the port city three times in the fourteenth century and again in the fifteenth century, and in 1474 the Marseilles city council asked Michel Merulle of Genoa to move to Marseilles to teach local artisans the principles of silk embroidery. By this time many needlework ateliers could be found in Marseilles, Avignon, Aix-en-Provence, and Arles, producing stitched and embroidered articles in cotton and silk, probably influenced by Italian work. Rambert cites fifteenth-century city commercial records showing exports throughout Provence and Italy, Spain, and Portugal of textile products in lengths and in finished clothing and domestic articles.

Provençal entrepreneurs' competitive pursuit of profitable foreign markets and aggressive investigation of wider opportunities was legendary. The Marseilles chamber of commerce, the oldest in the world, was organized in 1660 to foster port business. Its success in promoting finished textile activity near the close of the seventeenth century was astounding. Gaspard Carfeuil, hired by the chamber to document port business, reported an immense commercial needlework industry. In 1680, according to Carfeuil, five to six thousand women were employed in Marseilles ateliers to produce forty to fifty thousand pieces of *toiles piquées* (handstitched needlework articles) every year. These handstitched works were exported to other parts of France and to England, Hamburg, Holland, Italy, Portugal, and Spain.

Carfeuil's original report disappeared when Spanish invaders set fire to the Marseilles archives in one of many invasions, but a copy of the report was printed in 1783 in the *Encyclopédie méthodique: Commerce.* Other evidence corroborates the large scale of Marseilles needlework production and lends support to the image of thousands of women patiently engaged in fine stitchery for pay. Louis XIV's secretary of state, Jean-Baptiste Colbert, granted Marseilles the sole French franchise for receiving tax-free cotton textiles in 1669, in part to support the needlework industry. Katsumi Fukasawa in *Toilerie et commerce du Levant d'Alep à Marseille* reports enormous quantities of textiles imported to Marseilles from India and the Near East in the seventeenth and eighteenth centuries, specifically

for additional manufacturing: "*Mousselines,* also known as *cambresines,* were imported by Marseilles merchants and were used for bonnets, aprons, and other accessories of women. *Lisats,* white cotton weaves of fine quality from India, were used in the making of bedcovers stitched in Marseilles." These are the materials used for what is called *broderie de Marseille,* the corded, quilted work that encased narrow cording between two layers of cloth and was produced in port-city ateliers by professionals.

Carfeuil notes specifically that the *toiles piquées* were "worked in Marseilles"; they were not imported from other regions for re-export. This clarification is relevant to quilt research because at the same time that Carfeuil documented the high level of Marseilles-produced quilted work, there was apparently another source of similar needlework: the Portuguese colony at Goa on the west coast of India. Averil Colby in *Quilting* discusses seventeenth-century Indo-Portuguese quilting that features motifs of human figures, animals, birds, ships at sail, and other pictorial quilted images achieved by corded needlework using colored silk textiles. Surviving examples include a peach-colored silk quilt with motifs of hunting scenes and a ship in full sail, found at Truro in Cornwall, England, and documented by the Quilters' Guild, and a reversible blue-and-pink silk "Hunters Quilt" with motifs of hunting scenes attributed to Goa about 1700 and now in the collection of the Los Angeles County Museum of Art.

Although both the Marseilles and the Indo-Portuguese needlework traditions used a corded quilting technique and produced articles for commercial markets, there are marked differences between the two traditions. Marseilles quilting of the seventeenth and eighteenth centuries was worked primarily (although not exclusively) in fine cotton and featured an almost completely filled ground; any empty spaces between the entwined flowers, birds, animals, human figures, monograms, and other motifs were generally filled in with parallel lines of cording. The work attributed as Indo-Portuguese, in contrast, has many empty spaces between motifs, perhaps because the more fragile silk fabrics could not be overworked, lest the fibers split.

Tantalizing mention of the nature of Marseilles needlework is made in the 1660 chamber of commerce record of a gift to Madame Bellinzani, the wife of Secretary Colbert's first deputy, of "six pieces of *cambresine* filled with flowers . . . and three quilted petticoats bought from M. François Picquet, at the price of ten pistoles," according to d'Agnel. The brief reference does not indicate whether the flowers on the *cambresine* pieces were modeled in the corded needlework known as *broderie de Marseille* or whether they were printed on the cotton cloth. For while one group of Marseilles entrepreneurs was pursuing profits from needlework production, another group was organizing yet another textile industry: the production of cottons printed with pretty motifs.

A GOLD SILK BEDCOVER dating from about 1770 and made from taffeta woven in Avignon is suffused with corded and quilted motifs often found in Provençal broderie de Marseille, including marguerites, or daisies, framed by tessellated diamond shapes.

Captivating Cotton Indiennes

In the first years of the seventeenth century Marseilles received abundant quantities of a dazzling "new" textile. *Indiennes* were cottons covered with colorful painted and printed flowers, mythic scenes, illustrated poems, and amazing exotic scenes with flowering trees and wondrous animals. Imported from India (hence the name), where colorfast dying techniques had been perfected, these painted and printed cottons caused a textile revolution in Europe. They were used decoratively for curtains, wall coverings, and of course bedcovers and fashionable garments. Articles made of these cottons were washable, comfortable, and pretty and compared favorably with those made of silk, linen, wool, and particularly hemp, which was inexpensive but scratchy and difficult to dye.

Indelible colors were achieved by the use of mordants, chemical agents that caused the dyes to adhere to cotton. At first mordants were brushed on the fabric by hand. Later mordants were applied with printing blocks carved of wood. Multiple colors were obtained by using a series of separate blocks, one for each color, or by hand painting additional (nonfast) dyes on the textile. The terms "painted" and "printed" in reference to early floral-motif cottons are used fairly interchangeably.

Alice Beer in *Trade Goods: A Study of Indian Chintz* quotes Duarte Barbosa, a Portuguese traveler who wrote enthusiastically from Cambay in western

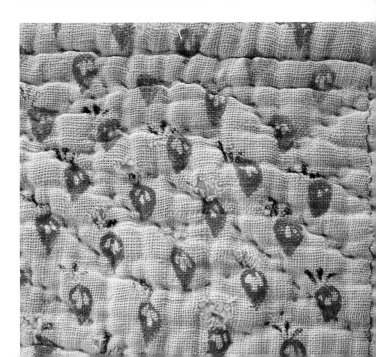

India in 1516: "They also make here very beautiful quilts and testers of beds finely worked and painted and quilted articles of dress." Many countries battled over trade access to these coveted textiles, with the Dutch and English emerging as the most successful in the seventeenth century. To give themselves a competitive edge, in 1662 the directors of the British East India Company supplied European patterns to Indian cotton painters for them to copy.

In *Printed French Fabrics: Toiles de Jouy,* Josette Brédif writes that in 1648 Benoît Ganteaume, a local card printer, and Jacques Baville, a local engraver, joined forces to print their own cotton cloth, an entrepreneurial move consistent with the Marseilles tradition of emulating the success of others. Their venture spawned other local textile print shops, and within a short period of time needleworkers had access to Marseilles-produced cotton prints, also dubbed *indiennes.* Cardinal Jules Mazarin, the notorious prime minister to the young Louis XIV, owned a quilted bedcover of locally printed *indiennes* in 1653. The description of this bedcover proves that it was also quilted locally; Beaumelle notes that the backing was of *cotonine,* a weave that combined cotton thread from India and hemp from Burgundy, produced only in Marseilles.

During his reign (1643–1715) Louis XIV charged his talented secretary of state, Colbert, with increasing the grandeur of the state—and presumably its coffers. Colbert enticed Eastern textile dyers to settle in Marseilles and bring the secrets of their colorfast dyes with them. He granted Marseilles the sole right to import cotton textiles tax free, thereby reducing the cost of materials necessary for both the white cotton *broderie de Marseille* and the infant cotton printing industry. Colbert then turned his attention to expanding export markets, with the full cooperation of aggressive Marseilles merchants. Their pretty gift of flowered *cambresines* to Madame Bellinzani, mentioned earlier, was perhaps a shrewd move to advance their commercial prospects. Gaston Rambert in the sixth volume of his *Histoire du commerce de Marseille* wrote that in 1670, when Madame Bellinzani's husband ordered the ship captain Nicolas Arnoul to begin trade with the French colonies in North America, he required the captain to take Marseilles *"toiles de bonne qualité"* (good-quality Marseilles textiles), along with the barrels of Provençal wine, olives and olive oil, and figs and raisins to offer in exchange for sugar cane. Active textile trade was quickly established with French colonists in Martinique and Guadeloupe.

THE PRINTED AND PAINTED COTTON TOP of this small quilt (34 × 50 inches) (above), dating to the late seventeenth or early eighteenth century, shows an improbable combination of Indian and European pattern motifs. The principal composition is much like an Indian prayer rug, yet the floral swags across the bottom are typically European.

DETAILED ANIMAL FIGURES *grace the printed toile "Les quatre parties du monde," designed by Jean-Baptiste Huet in about 1785 (below). This print was one of the fine printed fabrics produced by the famed Oberkampf textile factory at Jouy-en-Josas, near Paris, from 1760 to 1843.*

SCENES OF LOVERS *from mythological and biblical sources are depicted in an early-nineteenth-century quilted toile (opposite). Among the scenes are Psyche awakening Amour, "le mouton cheri," Angelique and Medo, and a graceful bather, perhaps Bathsheba.*

40

*FORBIDDEN INDIENNES were impossible for the fashionable French
to resist during the prohibition of printed cottons. An array
of eighteenth-century French printed cottons, displayed on iron and wire
doll beds (opposite), shows the allure of these pretty but practical textiles.*

Prohibition

By the last quarter of the seventeenth century both the all-white *broderie de Marseille* and colorful *indiennes* were in high fashion and high demand. Articles stitched in *broderie de Marseille* were ordered by royal houses throughout Europe. The pretty *indiennes*—quilted into bedcovers and small throws, mounted as wall coverings, draped over windows, and fashioned into comely frocks, dressing gowns, and other garments—had captured the imagination of the beau monde. Even the middle class had money and taste enough to acquire the fancy white work and the charming prints. In Molière's *Le bourgeois gentilhomme* (1670), Monsieur Jourdain wears a chamber robe of *indienne*. Octave Teissier in *Meubles et costumes XVI–XVIIIème siècles* cites the inventory of Louis XIV's general treasurer, Jean de Layat, who possessed a bedcover made of an *indienne* print bordered with Chinese satin. Clearly, these Marseilles-produced cotton textiles were usurping much of the market formerly enjoyed by French manufacturers of silk, velvet, tapestry, and woolens.

This was too much for other textile industrialists to bear, and powerless they were not. They had friends in court whom they lobbied fiercely to hobble their competitors. Their victory came on October 26, 1686, when the council of state prohibited the importation and local production of white and printed cotton cloth throughout France, a ban that would last until 1759. To avoid throwing thousands of people out of work, Marseilles merchants were still permitted to import white toiles into Marseilles for the needlework and printing industries. But the resulting products had to be either exported or used only in Marseilles; they were not to be sold within France. It may have been mere coincidence or perhaps an attempt at bribery that nine days before this decree the Marseilles chamber of commerce presented a grand gift of *toiles piquées* to France's director general of commerce, Monsieur de Lagny, "in recognition of the good services that this high official freely gives to our commerce on all occasions," a paean cited by Louis Chabaud in *Marseille et ses industries*.

The kingdom-wide prohibition against the domestic sale of *broderie de Marseille* and locally

*PARISIANS WHO DARED TO DEFY Louis XV's 1730 prohibition against wearing printed
cottons were subject to a fine of 200 livres, confiscation of the illegal garments, and public
humiliation. A police announcement (above), dated July 29, 1730, was read publicly
before being posted throughout Paris and identifies offenders by name and address.*

printed *indiennes* did not stanch the consumer appetite for them. When the first laws prohibiting sales of printed cloth proved ineffective, additional ordinances were issued and reissued in various forms to try to stop consumption. Finally ordinances were passed forbidding the wearing of printed cloth. But the mode for printed fabrics was no passing fancy. Printers continued printing, and stubborn consumers flagrantly disobeyed the law. Police action was demanded. Parisians caught flaunting gowns of printed *indiennes* were stripped of their frocks. In 1730, several decades after the first laws were passed, informers peered through the windows of private homes to catch clerks and ladies' maids garbed in desirable contraband. Lawbreakers faced hefty fines and were further humiliated by having their names printed on public posters.

Yet the fashion for garments and decor made of prohibited textiles survived. Twice during the ban the duke of Villars accepted gifts of *toiles piquées* from Marseilles businessmen, according to Beaumelle. Court ladies paraded their *indiennes* frocks in their country chateaus. Henri Clouzot relates in *Painted and Printed Fabrics* that the flamboyant Madame de Pompadour, mistress of Louis XV—the king whose law it was—furnished her whole apartment and significant parts of her wardrobe with *indiennes.*

Despite the allure of the illegal textiles, Marseilles production of both *broderie de Marseille* and printed cottons eventually dropped by one-third. Marseilles

was further devastated by *la peste* (the plague) of 1720, which was carried to the port city from Syria on the ship *Le Grand Saint-Antoine,* captained by J. B. Chataud. Although several sailors had died of disease en route, the ship evaded quarantine and officials claimed that the deadly disease was transmitted by the cargo of cotton cloth, according to Rambert. Fifty thousand Marseillais died, and all importation of cotton was banned. Until the end of the prohibition in 1759, the few remaining Marseilles needlework ateliers and textile print works produced goods only for the West Indies, the small remaining European markets, and, defiantly, for French entrepreneurs willing to trade in contraband.

In *Almanach historique de Marseille,* Georges Grosson, a local eighteenth-century historian, wrote that in 1723 Marseilles was producing cotton fabrics called *herbages* that imitated Indian prints but were better "in beauty and quality." Chamber of commerce records of 1733 show the existence of twenty-four local cotton print works in that year. In 1744, Chabaud notes, Jean-Rodolphe Wetter employed seven hundred men and women to make printed cottons designed by artists hired straight from the Marseilles painting academy. Wetter later went bankrupt, but other scofflaw Provençal printers set up shop in his place.

Forbidden legal access to domestic markets in decorative cottons, Marseilles merchants also sought profits in silk textile production, adopting techniques

"How women yearn for things forbidden."

François Rabelais, *Gargantua et Pantagruel,* Book III (1545)

of high-quality silk weaves produced in the famous Lyons factories. Joseph Fabre created the first major Marseilles silk works in 1685; other manufacturers followed suit. According to Paul Masson in *La Provence au XVIIIème siècle,* by 1730 sixty weavers were employed to produce gold- and silver-colored specialty silk goods. Marseilles silk weavers never attained the sophistication of those in Lyons because their raw materials were not as refined, but Marseilles-produced silks, known as *bourrettes,* were still desirable. Woven from the rougher outer fibers of the silkworm's cocoon, *bourrettes* were strong and resistant to wear; they were thus particularly suitable for garments and bedcovers that received a great deal of use.

The seventeenth and eighteenth centuries were a fertile period for the textile arts of Provence. Professionally stitched *broderie de Marseille* articles captivated Europe and launched a tradition of finely articulated corded, stuffed, and quilted all-white work that continued in Provence for two hundred years. Colorful printed cottons, first imported from India and subsequently imitated in Provençal print works, charmed their way into the wardrobes and domestic decor of all France. Jealous silk manufacturers found competition from both finely stitched quilted works and pretty printed cottons so threatening to their business that they successfully lobbied the king to prohibit sales of these two luxury cotton products within France. Yet the public taste for decorative cotton textiles in France endured.

TWO LATE-EIGHTEENTH-CENTURY QUILTS were made from fabrics printed in Provence. A Provençal bedcover filled with kashmir cones and stylized flowers at left reflects the Provençal taste for strong colors, while a bedcover at right made from an indigo-and-white woodblock print features leafy fronds and pomegranates.

Embroidery from Within

A STUFFED BRODERIE DE MARSEILLE WEDDING QUILT *reflects the same high sculptural relief as the white marble fountain in which it is placed. For both objects form is revealed through the play of light over their surfaces.*

MAGINE A SNOWY WHITE BEDCOVER *covered with finely articulated flowers, trailing boughs, entwined herbs, and garlands—a luxurious garden all in white. The play of light and shadow over the surface illuminates each curve and arc of the raised pattern. This bedcover is the stuff of dreams, and thousands of them were fashioned by mistresses of the needle in Marseilles two hundred years ago and earlier for the beds of European aristocrats. The French refer to this elegant textile art as "embroidery from within."*

A CENTRAL MEDALLION filled with an elaborate crowned monogram and framed by floral scrolls further embellished with French knots dominates an eighteenth-century broderie de Marseille bedcover (above). MORNING SUNLIGHT delineates surface relief in a superb early-eighteenth-century broderie de Marseille bedcover (opposite).

Corded White Work

All-white bedcovers handstitched in corded *broderie de Marseille* were among the finest pieces produced by professional needle-women in Marseilles ateliers in the seventeenth and eighteenth centuries. Success with *broderie de Marseille* depended on an ability to work skillfully in three dimensions. The needleworker had to raise defined lines of relief on what was otherwise a flat, monochromatic surface. The women who created *broderie de Marseille* were artists and artisans who had full mastery of their specialty. They understood the prop-

erties of light: if the surface relief of a textile was manipulated, light would reveal pattern. High areas would be brighter, while lower areas would recede into shadow. In addition, the high-quality textiles to which these women had access enhanced the reflection of light. Their facility with the needle is beyond doubt.

The materials for the glorious seventeenth- and eighteenth-century *broderie de Marseille* were few and simple: cotton fabric, slim cording, and thread. The surface textile was a fine, long-staple cotton percale, the underside a looser-weave cotton. Small, almost imperceptible stitches joined top to bottom along lines of a pattern to form narrow interior channels. Slender cord-

ing was drawn through these channels to raise the pattern in surface relief and give the work flexibility. Charles Germain de Saint-Aubin, appointed designer of the royal wardrobe by Louis XV, described the technique in his 1770 book *L'art du brodeur:*

La broderie de Marseille is made with small stitches in white thread around the contours of compartments or flowers drawn in white on the batiste or mousseline doubled onto another stronger cloth, both stretched on an ordinary frame. When all objects are thusly stitched, one turns the frame over, then with a pointed object, or the head of a large pin, one inserts more or less cotton cording between the two fabrics, through a little hole made in the back of each flower, to give it relief. When one has thusly filled all objects, taking care not to puncture the batiste or mousseline, one turns the frame over again. Then one fills the ground of the design with little knots made with the needle [French knots], one after another closely set, which produces a textured ground and agreeably trims the flowers, especially for toilette furnishings.

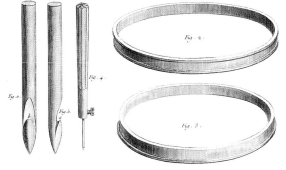

Saint-Aubin omitted a critical step in his instructions. The small stitches delineating the pattern contours had to be made in double lines, parallel to each other, to hold the cording in place. If the stitching lines were not precisely parallel or if they meandered off line or were set too far apart, the cording would not round out the channels and no clear surface pattern would emerge. When done skillfully, patterns in *broderie de Marseille* stood out in sharp outline. The

effect was subtle and elegant, and the finished piece was supple and strong. Despite the fragile appearance of the floral motifs, these corded pieces could withstand much washing and wear.

The basic design repertoire of *broderie de Marseille* featured intricate floral forms: swags, garlands, vines, entwined herbs, thistles, leafy branches, and flowers that meandered from urns and vases in lush profusion. *Broderie de Marseille* needlework depicted symbols of prosperity and social status—monograms set within a scrolled frame, ropes of pearls—and often included cunning depictions of human figures, birds, winged insects, and hares, deer, and other animals. The

ONE-HALF OF A CORDED LINEN WAISTCOAT (below) from the eighteenth-
century American colonies was worked with a needlework technique identical
in all respects to the finest examples of broderie de Marseille, even to the
detail of French-knot embroidery, and is most likely a French import.

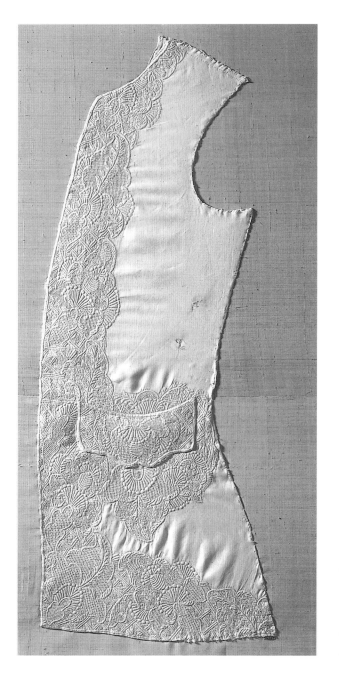

symmetrical balance seen in almost all surviving pieces points to use of a detailed, well-conceived plan, which was traced or chalked on the fabrics before the first stitch was made.

The corded, stuffed "Tristram" bedcover made in Sicily about 1395 (see pages 30–31) has withstood the ravages of time and remains an example of the possible roots of the technique and the patterns used in *broderie de Marseille*. The figurative panels in "Tristram" are more pictorial than most surviving pieces of Marseilles-made corded needlework. However, an eighteenth-century bedcover in a private collection in Perpignan, Provence, like "Tristram," illustrates battle, hunting, and other figurative scenes in corded needlework, although no figures are stuffed. Two features of the Perpignan bedcover, typical of Provence, reveal its French origin: the central pattern includes a vase of flowers, and monograms grace each corner.

Bedcovers made in all-white, corded *broderie de Marseille* were magnificent. As large as one hundred inches square to reach the floor on each side of raised eighteenth-century beds, they were lavishly worked in miniature relief. Most eighteenth-century *broderie de Marseille* bedcovers incorporate a central motif, such as a vase of flowers or a medallion formed of initials set under a crown. This central figure is framed by interlocking scrolls, wreaths, or a series of leafy garlands, from which floral branches, vines, and ropes of herbs trailed. Every inch was filled with figures, and

THE MASTERY OF PROFESSIONAL PROVENÇAL NEEDLEWOMEN is displayed in an eighteenth-
century broderie de Marseille bedcover bordered with a hand-knotted fringe
(opposite). Every inch of cloth is filled with raised design—monograms and vases of
flowers on a field of scrolls and floral trails, each flower garnished with French knots.

each piece required needlework precision—to plan the desired composition, transfer designs to the fabric, stitch the narrow channels (working at ten or more stitches to the inch), and finally draw the cording through the channels to realize the pattern. Large bedcovers must have taken at least several hundred hours to complete and perhaps were worked by several professional needlewomen. The products of this painstaking labor must have been costly.

Similar *broderie de Marseille* patterns were applied to *couvre-pieds, chauffoirs,* and articles of clothing, including elegant undergarments for the wealthy and even tiny clothes for infants of noble birth. By the end of the seventeenth century demand for *broderie de Marseille* came from all over Europe and provided employment for thousands of professional needlewomen in Marseilles ateliers.

The small throw known as a *couvre-pieds* was described by Madame de Genlis, a member of the eighteenth-century French elite, as quoted by Marie-José Beaumelle in *Les arts décoratifs en Provence:* "When one rested on a chaise longue, one always had a *couvre-pieds.* Decency required it, because there reclining, the least movement can uncover one's feet and even one's legs. Moreover, a beautiful *couvre-pieds* is an elegant sort of dress." Pierre Verlet in *La maison du XVIIIème siècle en France* published a 1779 inventory of the winter furnishings of the duchess of Bourbon's bedchamber in the Palace of Bourbon, which showed that the duchess had a large "*couvre-pied en picqure [sic] de Marseille.*" In about 1750 Queen Marie Lescynska, the wife of Louis XV, redecorated her bedroom at Fontainebleau with three large and three small *couvre-pieds de Marseille,* eighteen matching pillows, and twelve dozen *chauffoirs* worked in *broderie de Marseille,* according to Beaumelle.

A *chauffoir* was another requisite luxury, defined by Antoine Furetière in his 1690 *Dictionnaire universel* as a small throw or undergarment that is first warmed in an oven and then tucked around one's self—a luxurious antidote to the drafts and chills in chateaus with high ceilings and no central heating. *Chauffoirs* of *broderie de Marseille* served a singular purpose when a noblewoman was "lying in." When labor commenced, her attendants would lay a dozen or more heated *chauffoirs* on her abdomen. The heat and weight and perhaps even the beautifully stitched symbols of abundance were thought to ease and encourage delivery of a well-born infant.

Men, women, children, and even babies from wealthy families had garments fashioned of corded *broderie de Marseille.* Annie Roux in *Le textile en Provence* wrote that the 1700 inventory of Seigneur J. de Gravier listed three nightcaps, a stomacher, and a toilette towel of this exquisite work. When the chevalier Roze died in 1733, he left two *broderie de*

LIKE MANY EUROPEAN ARISTOCRATS, Louise-Marie Thérèse Bathilde d'Orleans, duchess of Bourbon, indulged her fondness for Provençal textiles. Her bedroom decor changed with the season—crimson silk bed hangings and quilted covers in winter, opalescent silk furnishings and quilted covers trimmed in ribbons in summer.

AN EIGHTEENTH-CENTURY BRODERIE DE MARSEILLE COUVRE-PIEDS, *lushly worked in stylized floral forms, rests on a French slipper chair. Some French textile historians believe that surviving pieces found in Provence, as this one was, may not have met quality standards for exportation, although they appear to be finely worked.*

Marseille corsets, according to Beaumelle. Women's wardrobes held *broderie de Marseille* camisoles, corsets, bonnets, and pockets that were worn separately, tied around the waist under skirts. At the Gard archives is a record dated February 19, 1754, of the dowry Gabrielle Fornier of Nîmes brought to her marriage to Etienne David Maynier; it included a toilette towel and a *jupon* (skirt), both described as *"piqué de Marseille."* Antoine Raspal painted dozens of portraits of stylish women, rendering their garments in delightful detail and thus allowing us to see how articles of *broderie de Marseille* were incorporated into fashionable costumes. One extraordinary piece was a long-sleeved corset, laced with cording dyed indigo blue to enhance the effect of the stitched pattern.

How luxurious for European aristocrats to adorn themselves in hand-decorated white undergarments, enhance their toilette tables with towels stitched in ornate floral motifs, cover their silk-clad ankles with elegant white corded throws as they reclined, and delight in snowy white confections of intertwined flowers and herbaceous forms covering their beds. So attractive were these luxuries that jealous silk manufacturers took measures to stop their production, resulting in a prohibition against the sale of *broderie de Marseille* articles within France from 1686 to 1759 (see pages 43–45). Yet *tapissiers* (professional needlework ateliers) continued to produce fine work for legal export to other European countries and the French Caribbean colonies.

*SOPHISTICATED DESIGN FORMS achieved by modeling fine white percale
with tiny stitches and compartments of cotton batting are revealed in three Provençal
wedding quilts of the late eighteenth and early nineteenth centuries (opposite).*

Stuffed White Work

During the eighteenth century the technique of *broderie de Marseille* was enlarged in scale and more commonly included stuffed work techniques, in which pattern compartments were filled with bits of cotton batting to raise design elements even higher and make them more rounded on the finished surface than could be accomplished with cording. The "Tristram" bedcover contained elements of stuffed work, but surviving articles worked in *broderie de Marseille* from the first half of the eighteenth century hold only narrow cording. Characteristic of their creativity and skill, Provençal needlewomen had continued to explore ways to enhance pattern relief on the textile surface, and by midcentury bits of cotton batting inserted into the back of pattern compartments increased the surface definition of these compartments. Stuffing allowed larger, higher motifs to catch broader areas of light and darker shadows to form along recessed lines of stitching. The result was a more sculptural effect.

Needlewomen used the same textiles, a fine cotton percale on the top and a looser-weave cotton on the back. As in corded *broderie de Marseille,* a surface fabric and a lining fabric were basted together and set in a frame, the desired design was traced onto the top fabric, and lines of stitching through both fabrics followed pattern lines: two parallel lines where cording was to be inserted, single-line stitches to create compartments for cotton batting. When the entire design was stitched, the work was turned over, and cording and batting were inserted through small holes made by pushing aside the woven threads in the backing fabric. Cording could be drawn through channels with a blunt-pointed needle. Bits of cotton batting were less transigent and probably caught at the raw edges of the aperture. It must have taken extraordinary patience to work the exact amount of cotton batting into design cavities to create a rounded surface, firm and smooth to the touch. Once the piece was stuffed, backing threads were worked into their former positions, yet in surviving corded and stuffed *broderie de Marseille* textiles small tails of cotton cording and wisps of cotton batting show the point of insertion.

Articles of dress were artfully worked in stuffed, high-relief *broderie de Marseille,* especially camisoles and all-white *cotillons* (quilted petticoats). The young mademoiselle in Antoine Raspal's 1779 painting *Portrait de jeune fille en costume d'Arles* (see page 6) wears a quilted camisole of white *mousseline,* its neckline and sleeves bordered in a corded and stuffed pattern of puffed triangles and geometric designs. The border decor of *cotillons* was also successfully stitched in corded and stuffed *broderie de Marseille.* Even the most modest, plain-colored cotton *cotillon* made in this technique attracted attention because of the clear relief of its border design.

*A STUFFED WHITE WEDDING QUILT (pages 62–63), dating from
about 1850, displays a profusion of scrolled fruit and flower forms enclosing initials
(at left) and a bird of paradise on the wing above garlands of pineapples,
plums, melons, and ripe pomegranates (at right).*

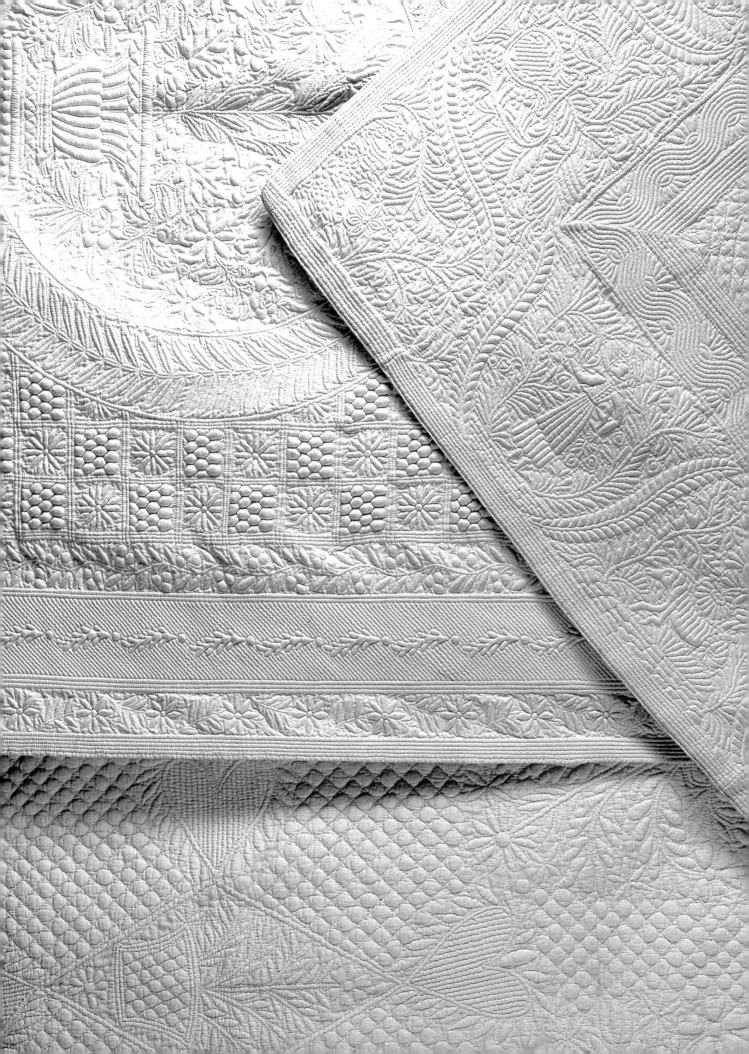

Fair Symbols for the Nuptial Bed

The art of corded and stuffed *broderie de Marseille* is most gloriously expressed in the Provençal tradition that called for creation of an all-white wedding quilt to grace the top of the marriage bed. The most magnificent wedding quilts were made to order by professional needlewomen, who often incorporated motifs of significance to the families. Corded and stuffed *broderie de Marseille* articles were fairly thick and stiff, which helped needlewomen achieve eye-catching, three-dimensional patterns. With such ability to draw attention, quilting motifs took on new significance and their repertoire expanded, drawing inspiration from a wealth of sources.

The motifs in wedding quilts provide a directory to eighteenth- and nineteenth-century *broderie de Marseille* designs, which went far beyond the stylized floral forms, garlands, and leafy vines seen earlier. Curves were spaced with geometric patterns of puffed diamonds and corded borders. Plants, flowers, and fruits indigenous to Provence served as models for quilting motifs, especially melons (to symbolize fertility), rosemary branches, laurel swags, marguerites (to symbolize femininity), sunflowers, grapes and grapevines, and thistles. Architectural motifs and even whole buildings were depicted in stuffing and stitches. The Maison Carrée, a classical Roman structure built in Nîmes in 100 B.C. and still standing, is the focal point of the corded and stuffed border of one wedding

64

THE MAISON CARRÉE IN NÎMES, *shown in an 1843 engraving (opposite bottom),*
is the best preserved of the first-century Roman temples still standing in Provence.
Flanked by heart-bearing cupids and sprays of rosemary, it appears in the border
of a wedding quilt attributed to early-nineteenth-century Nîmes (bottom).

quilt. Roman columns topped with flying disks distinguish another.

Figures of men and women in detailed dress frequently appeared, reminiscent of the corded and stuffed "Tristram" and "Alexander" pieces of the fifteenth century. Other motifs included birds, winged cherubs, sheep, and dogs bearing baskets of flowers. Traditional symbols of love, longevity, and abundance are seen in hearts, fountains of youth, and cornucopias. Classical motifs then fashionable throughout Europe included lyres and baskets, urns, and vases filled with flowers. Most fascinating were the depictions of current events and travelers' tales. The border of one wedding quilt holds a hot-air balloon bearing a wicker gondola, a hut topped with a windmill, and a tented canopy.

The creative level achieved in seventeenth- and eighteenth-century *broderie de Marseille* is remarkable. In essence, needlewomen created visually pleasing, highly detailed, three-dimensional decorative objects merely by manipulating monochromatic colored cloth and using only thread and a filling material. Despite its Italian roots and Indian design influences, neither Italy nor India can lay claim to the distinctly high art that was expressed in corded *broderie de Marseille* of the seventeenth century and corded and stuffed *broderie de Marseille* of the eighteenth century. It is little wonder that the glorious work of Marseilles professionals was sought throughout Europe— these quilted items were outstanding, and the skills required to accomplish them were difficult to imitate.

*white wedding quilt tradition. References are drawn from a variety
of folklore sources ranging from both the natural
and supernatural to current events and exotic travelers' tales.*

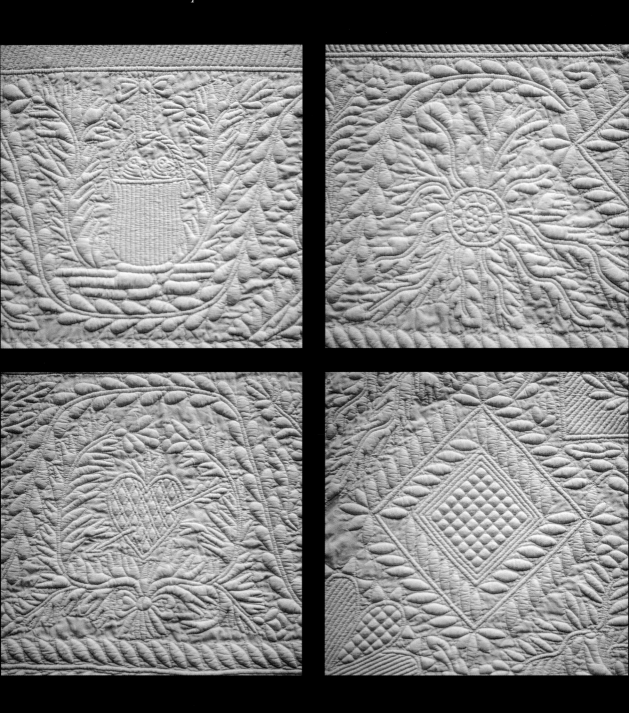

*Motifs of Provençal stuffed work include a pair of lovebirds snuggled
in a basket (top left), a blazing, even animate Provençal sun (top right),
a flaming heart pierced by the arrow of love and surrounded by rosemary swags
(bottom left), and a puffed diamond framed by laurel branches (bottom right).*

make up the border of a broderie de Marseille wedding quilt that dates
from 1770–1800. The scenes include a young woman in a laced corset (top left)
and a coquecigrue, a mythical half-beast, half-fish figure (top right).

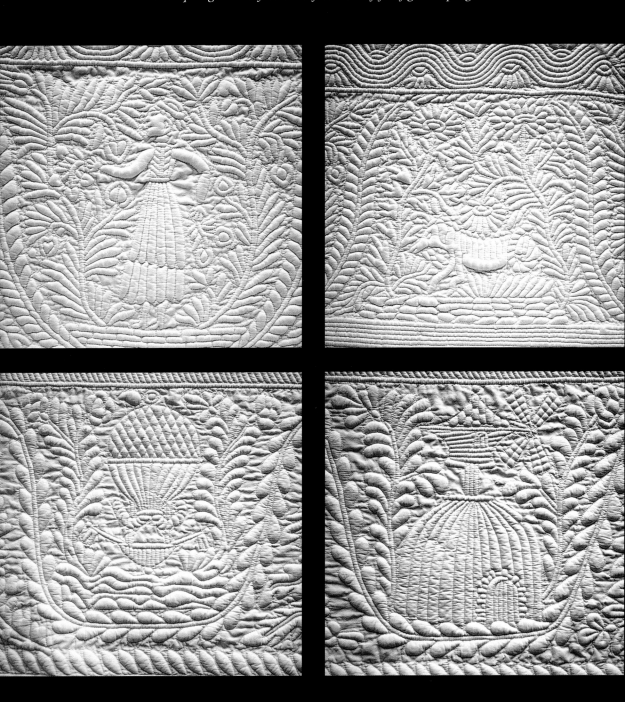

The first hot-air balloon in France ascended from the Tuileries in Paris in 1783,
so frightening residents of the nearby village of Gonesse that they shot it down.
A skillful needlewoman rendered a similar balloon (bottom left) as well as a windmill
(bottom right) in the border of a wedding quilt that dates from about the same decade.

Provençal Colors, Provençal Patterns

IN THE PROVENÇAL TRADITION, *a quilted bedcover hangs to air from an open window in the Villa Magalone in Marseilles. The quilt is made of a toile featuring large, brightly colored pineapples among floral motifs and was probably printed at Christophe-Philippe Oberkampf's famous print works in Jouy-en-Josas about 1785.*

"Adornment is never anything except a reflection of the heart."
Gabrielle (Coco) Chanel, "Remarks"

SPECIALLY IN PROVENCE, WHERE *nature provides abundant inspiration, flowers have been the most popular decorative motif for textiles. Provençal flowers bloom in all colors of the artist's palette—from spring's pale purple swags of wisteria to summer's golden sunflowers and crimson roses. Flowering trees and plants abound through all seasons except winter, and in winter they can be found indoors, blooming in decorative textiles covering a bed, thrown over a sofa, or stitched into quilted skirts, capes, vests, and other garments worn by the Provençals. Adept at the needle arts and eager to work with colorful plain and printed cottons and luscious silks, the women of Provence did not send all of their fine stitchery to the far corners of Europe. The open armoires and coffrets of Provençal households during the seventeenth and eighteenth centuries show how women brought summer bowers into their lives year-round.*

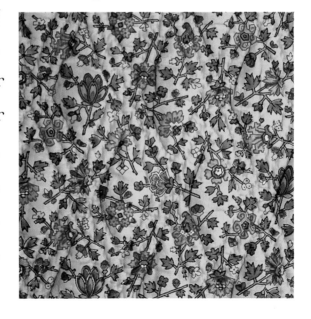

GOLD SILK BED FURNISHINGS *in the count's bedchamber of Château Grignan, near Orange (opposite), epitomize the luxurious appointments of seventeenth-century nobles in the days of Louis XIV.* A BÂTON ROMPUS, OR BROKEN RODS, PRINT *(above) mingles jagged branches with floral motifs and probably came from Jouy about 1807.*

Quilted, flower-patterned garments made practical and pretty sense against the bitter mistral wind that blows through three Provençal seasons. Market vendors as well as courtesans wore long quilted skirts called *jupons* or *cotillons,* stitched in gay floral prints or quilted in fanciful floral forms. Flower-strewn quilted throws and bedcovers looking like indoor gardens warded off the chill inside chateaus, farmhouses, and cottages alike.

The fine needlework produced in port-city ateliers was not limited to all-white cotton *broderie de Marseille.* Other luxury domestic and clothing articles were made of silk. A second *couvre-pieds* in the winter furnishings of the duchess of Bourbon's bedchamber (see page 54) was quilted of white satin. When richly colored silk and cotton were quilted in decorative patterns, the mottled light over the dimpled surface illuminated a range of dark and light hues. In *L'art du brodeur* Charles Germain de Saint-Aubin addresses the quilting technique of *toiles piquées:*

. . . after stretching the fabric one will use as the backing over a frame, one fully covers it with a carded light cotton batting; one covers this with the fine top cloth which one fixes tightly on the frame with pins all around; one lightly traces with chalk the scales, squares or mosaics that one wants to represent; one then follows the contour lines in little stitches of silk or cotton thread according to the cloth.

The art of Provençal plain quilting resided in the ability to raise pattern in high relief and produce patterns in pleasing compositions.

PROVENÇAL PRINTS IN SMALL FLORAL PATTERNS,
stripes, and bands of floral forms, quilted into bedcovers,
have long enlivened the interiors of modest homes.
These blue pieces date to the early 1800s.

Luxurious Silk Toiles Piquées

Fine quilted silk articles, probably first imported from China, India, and Italy and later domestically produced, were clearly regarded as luxury items. In 1564 members of the Marseilles chamber of commerce presented a quilted silk bedcover to Charles IX in honor of his first visit to Provence. In the third volume of *Histoire de commerce de Marseille* Raymond Collier writes that this silk piece was more valuable than the imported Persian rug that was also given to the king. Five years later chamber members gave the local ship captain Joseph Allenc several quilted silk bedcovers as a reward for improving port business.

Silk had been available in Marseilles since medieval times. Rough silk weaves called *bourrettes,* made from the outer strands of the silkworm cocoon, were produced locally. In the thirteenth century Italians from Lucca, just across the Mediterranean, supplied large amounts of Chinese silk to the annual trade fairs held in Champagne near Paris, as well as to Marseilles. By the fifteenth century merchants in Lucca exported their own woven silk textiles to Europe and India; Collier notes that Portuguese adventurers were surprised to find silk from Lucca in Calcutta in 1502. Ludovico di Varthema, a Portuguese who traveled through India from 1502 to 1508, described fifty ships a year leaving Bengal in India with silk and cotton "stuffs" bound for ports on the eastern Mediterranean and Aegean

Seas, where it could be relayed to Marseilles, according to Alice Beer in *Trade Goods.*

Woven silk production can be traced to fourteenth-century France, in Avignon, Paris, and a few other sites. At the beginning of the sixteenth century high-quality silk weaves were produced in the factories in Lyons and were soon renowned for their beauty. Woven silks featured stripes, small floral patterns, scrolls, and figured bands of the minutest detail.

Bountiful Cotton Toiles Piquées

Seventeenth- and eighteenth-century cotton prints came in a wide range of colors, scales, and motifs, from the simple to the complex, although most retained vestiges of the imported, floral print cotton *indiennes* designs. With the profusion of printed textile manufacturers came technological advances. Carved blocks of hardwood had been used in early printing and continued to be used to make *chafarcanis,* charming, small-scale, one- or two-color prints on coarsely woven white cotton, first imported from India and among the first to be imitated in Provence. The variety of *chafarcani* designs included little blossoms and buds, spotted stripes, and kashmir cone shapes set in simple order, for example, rows of red flowers between red stripes on a white ground, or a small red-and-brown floral sprig repeated on white.

More finely detailed prints were obtained by inserting copper blades and points in the wooden blocks to create designs such as a trailing floral stem or a flower's pistil. Even more complex prints were made from all-copper blocks by 1770 and from copper rollers by the end of the eighteenth century. Among the most popular prints in Provence were *herbages* prints, showing fields of small, bright flowers on a white or colored ground; *écailles imbriquées* prints, showing overlapped scales filled with small floral

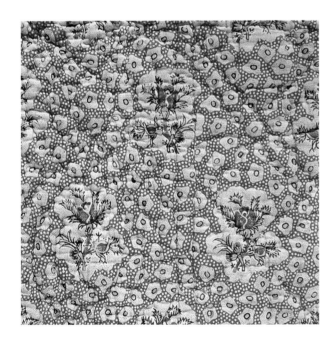
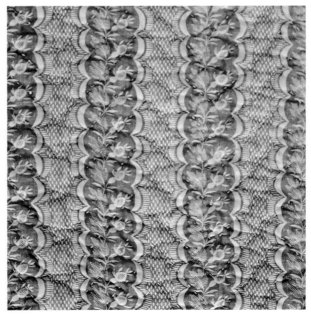

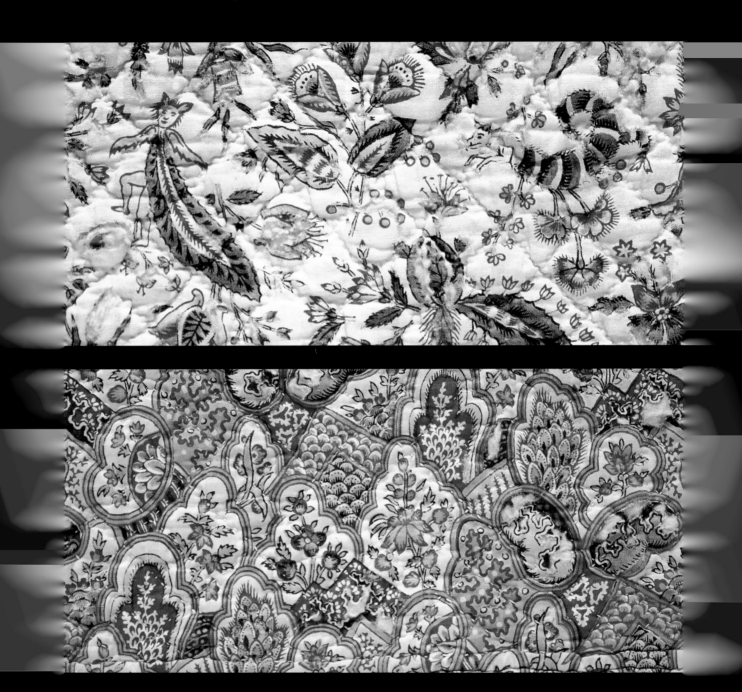

THE COQUECIGRUE, A MYTHICAL CREATURE *that was said to cause passersby to itch and squirm, took the form of animated leaves and flowers in a Jouy cloth from about 1790 (below).* ÉCAILLES IMBRIQUÉES, OR OVERLAPPING SCALES (bottom), *show Chinese influences in their coral branches, floral sprays, and feather plumes.*

ANGULAR BRANCHES MINGLED WITH BRIGHTLY COLORED BLOSSOMS *in prints called bâtons rompus (opposite) were always popular in Provence. The charming patterns and sparkling colors brightened winter bedchambers, and the batting within kept dreamers snug.*

forms; and *bâtons rompus* prints, showing small, articulated broken rods. In 1771 Georges Grosson, a Marseilles historian, observed that the printed cottons of Marseilles were "as beautiful as those of India in their regularity and good design."

Despite the seventy-year French prohibition against printed cottons, from 1686 to 1759, during the eighteenth century there was an abundant supply of them and of woven, patterned silks. Ateliers in Marseilles and other Provençal towns defied the law and continued to produce prohibited cottons. In the decades just before and after the prohibition was lifted, bright, printed cottons proliferated in newly established print works in Orange and other parts of Provence and in other areas of France, such as Beautiran, Nantes, Paris, and Rouen, and in Mulhouse, then a free city belonging to the Swiss confederation, now a part of France.

In 1760 Christophe-Philippe Oberkampf established one of the most successful of all cotton print factories in Jouy-en-Josas, near Paris, the source of the renowned *toiles de Jouy*. Oberkampf's textile designers were artists recruited from the finest arts academies in France; he hired highly skilled workers and used fine-quality raw materials and textiles. He also paid close attention to scientific progress and new research to ensure colorfast products. Beginning with the first meters of cloth to come from his print works, Oberkampf imitated and refined the most popular patterns of the time.

Many of the dye stuffs used to tint these textiles were derived from local flora and fauna. *Baiso-ma-mio,*

PLEASANT, RUSTIC SCENES *(opposite) were popular about 1780 and were produced
copiously in Oberkampf's print works in Jouy-en-Josas.* TEXTILE DYERS ELICITED
RICH COLORS *from natural products for their woodblock prints: golden yellow (below,
top) from various sources, reds (middle) from madder, and blue (bottom) from indigo.*

the golden, slightly mustard color so characteristic of
Provence, came from a variety of wild sumac called
grain d'Avignon and from flowering broom, saffron,
and sunflower petals. Flaming scarlet was made with
kermes, a local insect. Other dye colors, such as co-
chineal, another insect product that created a rich
scarlet, were imported; some of these were later grown
domestically. Recipes using the madder plant produced
a range of colors from cherry red to mauve, purple,
aubergine, and even black. Brazilwood produced a subtle red-brown. Indigo, oak gall, and pastel were the raw
materials for various hues of blue.

The rainbow of regional and imported dyes resulted in a wealth of plain-colored as well as fanciful
printed and woven silks and cottons. Because the
decorative effect of an article made from a printed
cotton or fancy woven silk was inherent in the two-
dimensional printed or woven pattern, quilting was a
secondary design element. Quilting patterns were usually simple line forms, such as diamond grids. More
fanciful quilting was sometimes stitched on the border, but the standard finish was one or more rows of
cording run through channels stitched through the
top and bottom fabrics at the edge. Quilting in the inner body of the piece retained warmth, and the corded
border resisted wear. Such simple construction meant
that the finished articles would be only as attractive as
the materials from which they were made. With lovely
textiles readily available, the results were almost always
pleasing, no matter how crude the stitching.

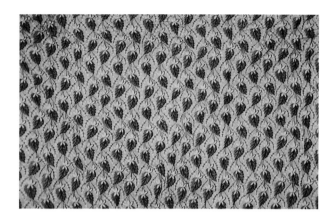

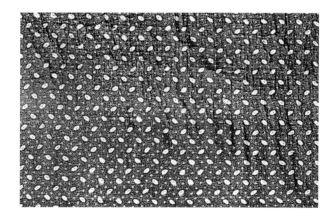

IN *"L'ATELIER DES PINCEAUTEUSES" (1764) (pages 84–85), J.G.M. Rosetti depicts the
workshop of Jean-Rodolphe Wetter's print works in Orange, opened in 1757. Under
Madame Wetter's watchful eye, young women handbrush additional colors on
woodblock prints known as toiles d'Orange, while her husband conducts business at left.*

Beauty and Warmth from Quilted Garments

In the beau monde of Provençal society, as in all others, the meanness or luxury of one's garments spoke volumes about one's place in the social hierarchy. There were many occasions on which to be seen and judged—saint's day festivals, Sunday promenades, weddings, christenings, receptions, and holidays. Fashion followed the dynamic changes in textile technology that brought greater variety, although sometimes at great cost. The many surviving costume pieces seem to indicate that Provençal women were infatuated with new textiles as they became available and incorporated them into their attire as much as their means allowed. A Provençal woman's social station in the eighteenth century could be quickly established by one glance at her *jupon*, the materials it was made of, and the quality of its stitching.

Jupons or *cotillons* were simple constructions of two long rectangles of cloth with batting held in between by lines of stitching. The top was gathered onto a twill tape to fit the waist, and the hem was reinforced by corded edging. Open slits at each side allowed access to separate pockets tied around the waist underneath the skirt. *Jupons* emphasized the female form—narrow at the waist and wide over the hips—while modestly concealing the legs. Quilting provided insulation against the fall, winter, and spring chill of the ever-blowing mistral wind and could also divert rays of a hot summer sun.

Women of modest means wore *jupons* and other garments made from *chafarcanis*, the simple one- or two-color floral prints that were relatively inexpensive yet comfortable and washable. The rude stitching in most of the surviving *jupons de chafarcanis*—large, somewhat crooked, and irregularly spaced—was probably done by nonprofessionals. Even the thread used to assemble these modest garments looks as if it had been unraveled from some other textile. Notoriously thrifty, Provençal women used and reused all textile products. *Chafarcani* prints already used for the outside of a quilted skirt frequently reappeared as a lining for another, the new material stitched on top of the old.

FLORAL MOTIFS PRINTED ON A FIELD OF CHOCOLATE BROWN, called ramoneur prints, were favored for men's and women's garments in the late eighteenth century. A rough brown silk droulet (below), a jacket with flying tails, was lined with an elegant floral ramoneur that still retains a surface glaze from its beeswax coating.

Wealthier women wore more elaborately figured and colored *jupons. Ramoneur* prints, showing multicolored flowers strewn on a dark brown field, were quilted into *jupons,* capes, and other garments and enjoyed long years of modishness in Provence. Because the combination of a busy floral print and a dark ground would obscure fancier quilting motifs, these printed cotton fabrics were usually stitched in diamond grid lines over a corded border.

During the period in which printed textiles were prohibited in France, a fashion for embroidered quilted goods arose. If fanciful flowers could not legally be printed on cloth, they could be embroidered, using colorful silk, cotton, or wool thread, most often on white cotton although also on white and colored silk. The result was so pretty that the fashion for quilted *toiles brochées,* with floral patterns stitched into the base fabric, and *pointe de Beauvais,* with floral patterns applied using a chain-stitch embroidery technique, lasted well beyond the end of the prohibition.

At the close of the eighteenth century every Provençal madame and mademoiselle who wore a *jupon jardinier* was in vogue. The *jardinier* print, sized just for *jupons,* featured delicate, multicolored arborescent trails in full bloom that extended from a luxuriant garden represented on the skirt's hem. Needlewomen, most likely professionals, quilted these fine-quality cotton skirts with tiny, closely set stitches, although the quilting pattern was still the

FIFTEEN ROWS OF CORDING HELPED A SKIRT (below) withstand wear
and create a bell-shaped garment. A grid of simple diamonds provided warmth.
HAND-EMBROIDERED FLORAL MOTIFS embellish two other jupons from
the 1700s (bottom), one using long stitches, the other with chain and satin stitches.

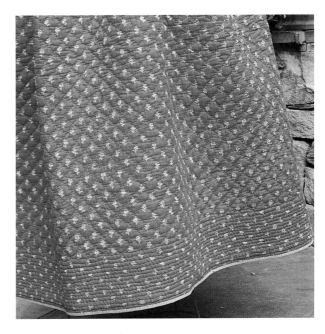

simple diamond grid on the body, edged with cording.

Silk fabric, although difficult to work with because of its fragility and slick surface, made beautiful quilted garments, whether stitched in *broderie de Marseille* or as a simple *toile piquée*. Octave Teissier in *Meubles et costumes XVI–XVIIIème siècles* cites the 1754 inventory of Madame Adrien Toudouze of Paris, who had a gown and matching *jupon* made of rose-and-white striped taffeta. Odile and Magali Pascal in *Histoire du costume d'Arles* mention the inventory of Thérèse Claret, who died in Arles in 1775 with four brilliantly colored, striped, and patterned silk *jupons* in her wardrobe. Quilted silk *jupons* were de rigueur for elegant occasions. Made to order for women of means, they were sumptuous garments, their borders frequently filled with motifs significant to the wearer.

A rose-colored silk *jupon* with all the earmarks of eighteenth-century needlework in the collection of the Musée de Château-Gombert in Marseilles confounds contemporary curators. The border of this elaborately decorated petticoat features a series of motifs recognizably linked to Provence—a sun with extended rays of light, flowers, hearts, and a giraffe, so clearly articulated it could not be anything else. Puzzled researchers find no evidence of giraffes in Provence until the nineteenth century, when the craze for information on exotic places was met with artists' works such as Nicholas Huet's 1827 *Study of the Giraffe Given to Charles X by the Viceroy of Egypt.*

JARDINIER PRINTS FILLED WITH LUXURIANT GARDENS reaching up from the skirt
hem were fashionable in the eighteenth century (pages 90–91). Rare images of
fountains grace the hem of the jupon jardinier on the left , while delicate, multicolored
arborescent trails reach from the hem to the waist of the one on the right.

89

"In bed we laugh, in bed we cry; And, born in bed, in bed we die.
The near approach a bed may show of human bliss to human woe."

Isaac de Benserade, *A son lit* (circa 1650)

Elegant Appointments for the Bedchamber

Quilted, colored silk textiles were used to splendid decorative effect in bedchambers. Gustave Arnaud d'Agnel in *L'ameublement Provençal et Comtadin durant le moyen âge et la Renaissance* cites the 1644 inventory of Monseigneur Louis de Bretel, archbishop of Aix-en-Provence, whose Red Bedroom held the following:

A walnut bed with three mattresses covered in white linen, hung with rose silk damask bed curtains edged in silk fringe, a headboard covered in blue silk taffeta with matching large quilted bedcover decorated with small balls of the same blue silk, bed skirts in the same blue silk, a blue silk velvet quilted cover with four decorative balls covered in the same silk velvet,

and placed on top of the bed, a small quilt made in red silk backed with green.

Colorful, even brilliant, quilted bedcovers and bed hangings have long been in high fashion in Provence and France. According to Marie-José Beaumelle in *Les arts décoratifs en Provence*, the 1757 inventory of Pierre Bouquin of Marseilles lists a *vanne piquée* of colorful *indiennes* from the Levant, bordered in green silk taffetas. (*Vanne* is the early French word for a small

quilted bedcover that rested on top of the bed.) In Marseilles emerald green signified wealth and fertility, and many bedcovers, particularly those made for the wedding bed, incorporated that color. Squire Bouquin's green-bordered *vanne* was made in the Provençal tradition called *fenêtre* (window) composition.

The modest addition of a wide border to a central textile is the only frequently encountered form of pieced work done in Provence. Simple diamond-grid quilting usually filled the body, but when a plain-colored fabric was used in the border, it was frequently stitched with decorative patterns. Typical border motifs were multiple-line cable forms and undulating parallel lines, although occasionally pieces show elaborate floral and vase motifs.

The *Encyclopédie méthodique: Commerce* (1783) emphasized the importance of the bed through its many references to bed furnishings. Its definition of the word "bed" focused on the craftsmen who made them *(menuisers)* as well as on those who furnished them *(tapissiers)* with mattresses, straw pallets, feather comforters, woolen coverlets, quilted covers, and *garniture*. The only definition of *garniture* refers to bed furnishings—curtains, upper and lower valances, canopy, and *courtepointe* (a quilted bedcover that originally fell to the floor but later did not extend below the lower valance, or bed skirt). All these furnishings

QUILTED PALE BLUE SILK *graces a bed (above) from the early 1800s.* WHEN MADAME DE SEVIGNÉ FIRST SAW THE CHÂTEAU GRIGNAN IN 1676, *she decried her daughter's lack of a bed: "It looks as if you lie on the bare floor with a cushion on your nose." When the chateau's decoration was completed (opposite), the count and countess indeed had a bed.*

consumed great quantities of plain and fancy textiles.

Class distinctions were obvious in the amount and quality of printed and woven decorative textiles used in bed furnishings. The deeper one's pockets, the more elegant the quilted bed hangings and accessories could be. In *Meubles et costumes* Teissier cites the inventory of Adrien Toudouze, a Parisian butcher who died in September 1754. Toudouze had a pleasant bedchamber, decorated with two pairs of white cotton curtains and a small couch upholstered in checked cotton. His bed had a high headboard, a canopy, and bed curtains of a brilliant woven iridescent silk trimmed with peach and yellow silk ribbons. His bed furnishings included a feather bolster and pillows, a white woolen coverlet, and a quilted bedcover of flower-print cotton.

In contrast, France's controller general of artillery, Garnier de Montigny, had more dramatic decor, according to a January 1758 inventory cited by Teissier. The general's curtains were long panels of cotton printed with large flowers on a red ground. As befits a military man, his small couch was a portable camp bed made of horsehair and leather strapping and covered with checked cotton. His bed had a curtained canopy, an upholstered headboard, doubled upper and lower valances, and a large quilted bedcover, all in a scarlet silk damask banded with gold. A small quilted bedcover in checked cotton rested on top.

Another genre of cotton prints used for quilted bed hangings and bedcovers was the large-scale prints representing scenic, allegorical, and historical figures. They became a high art of the Oberkampf factory's *toiles de Jouy* production because of its expertise with copper-plate and copper-roller printing. Cotton toiles in red on white, blue on white, and sepia on white found instant acceptance throughout France when they were introduced at the end of the eighteenth century. The success of these toiles was clearly evidenced by the vast number of imitations in other parts of France and England.

The seventeenth and eighteenth centuries were a fertile time for Provençal needle and textile arts. Locally printed cotton textiles proliferated in quantity and quality and were affordable to those of modest means. Woven silk goods in exotic patterns decorated the wardrobes and bedchambers of fine ladies. The colors and patterns had multiplied and flourished and added energy and creativity to the quilting tradition of Provence.

THE MYTHOLOGICAL TALE OF DIANE AND ENDYMION (opposite), was played out in red and white toile bed furnishings manufactured in Beautiran, near Bordeaux, about 1785. "LES COMÉDIENS AMBULANTS" (above), a scenic toile from Nantes printed around 1800, tells the story of itinerant players who entertained the Provençals.

On the World Stage

THE PROVENÇAL PAINTER ANTOINE RASPAL *was the son and brother of dressmakers in* Arles. *In his serene painting "*Madame Privat et ses deux filles*" (circa 1775), a sleeping baby is swaddled in a Provençal layette of white cotton or silk quilted in a diamond pattern—work that became treasured around the world.*

SUCH A FESTIVE OCCASION IT WAS: *the inauguration ball held on April 30, 1789, in New York City to celebrate the swearing in of George Washington as the first president of the United States of America. To this gala event women of the new republic wore their finest, most modish attire. They particularly sought to array themselves in the French taste to acknowledge French support of the American colonists' efforts during their War of Independence. Those who did not attend the ball could pore over newspaper and magazine accounts of the event. According to Elisabeth McClellan in "Historic Dress in America: 1607 to 1800," a "Colonel Stone" writing in "The Republican Court" described one frock: "One favorite dress was a plain celestial blue satin gown with a white satin petticoat." This artful woman enhanced her appearance à la française: a large gauze shawl bordered in satin*

QUILTED SILK PETTICOATS like the one worn by a young French woman in Gravelot's "Le lecteur" (mid-1700s) (above) were fashionable throughout Europe in the eighteenth century. POINTE DE BEAUVAIS (chain-stitch embroidery) worked over corded broderie de Marseille encircled women's skirts with whimsical garlands in the late 1700s (opposite).

98

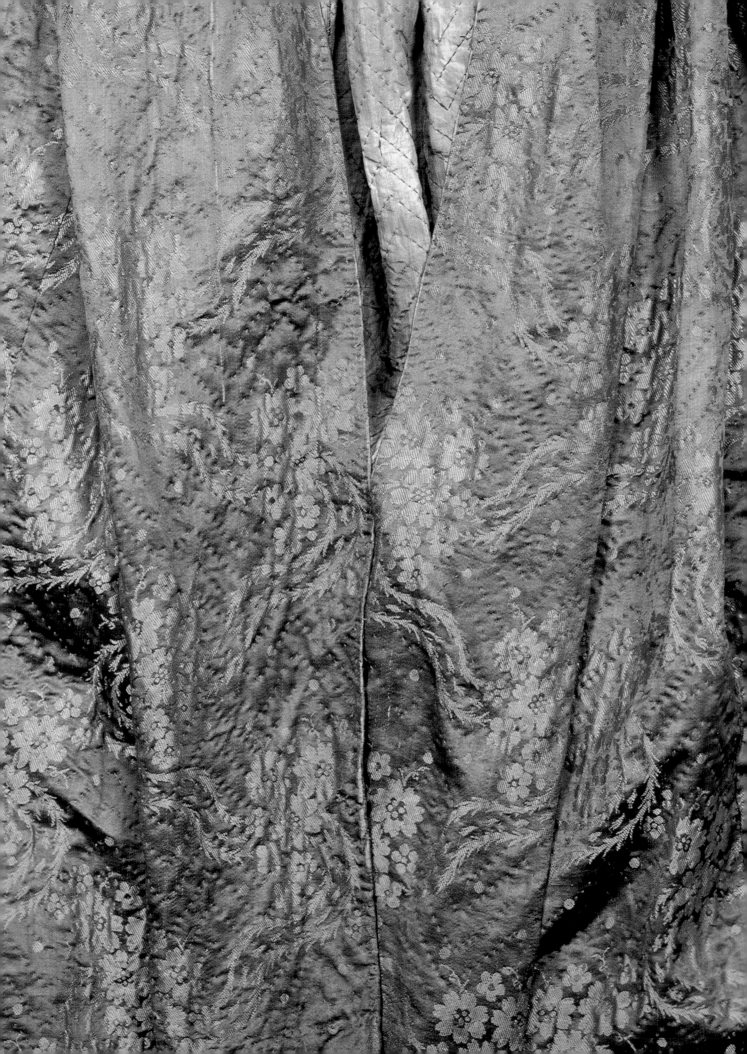

stripes was drawn over her shoulders, and she was coiffed in another "pouf of gauze, in the form of a globe" attached to a white satin headpiece with trailing garlands of artificial roses that mingled with curled locks at each side of her neck.

American women were not sacrificing popular taste to seek out garments reflecting French fashion, for Paris was then—as it had been since the mid-seventeenth century—the fashion leader for Europe and the Americas. Carl Kohler in *A History of Costume* writes that in the eighteenth century the fashion leadership of France was "unassailable," and illustrations of the latest styles were available in Paris as early as 1770 to serve as guides for dressmakers.

American enthusiasm for French culture and fashion during the years before and after the Revolutionary War cannot be overstated. Once independence from Britain was achieved, Americans were finally free to establish legal commercial access to French goods. The colonists' fascination with French products was based on intimate knowledge. Despite legal trade barriers erected by Britain to protect its own textile markets and monopolize trade with its American possessions, Londoners and colonists had traded in French goods through evasive and illegal means for the 150 years preceding American independence. Defiant sea captains, renegade privateers, and entrepreneurial Dutch intermediaries all played a role in provisioning Britain and the American colonies with luxury French products, especially textiles.

Recognition of this active underground trade opens new avenues in quilting research. Until now the American quilting tradition has been studied primarily in the context of its British roots. In *Silk Designs of the Eighteenth Century* Natalie Rothstein comments that "the Navigation Acts ensured that what the Colonies did import was English and not French." The trade barriers between Britain and France did not block importation of French needlework either to Britain or its colonies in North America. Close examination of quilted work that survives in Britain and the United States, even if not of Marseilles origin, raises the possibility of the influence of *broderie de Marseille.* Some pieces so resemble the corded and quilted wonders of Provence, with their twining floral forms, stylized flowers, diamond puff shapes, and completely covered ground, that the similarity raises questions about their attribution to origins other than Marseilles. Given the legal and illegal trade among France, Britain, and their colonies during the seventeenth and eighteenth centuries, the fine quilted needlework produced in Marseilles may well have been the direct ancestor of the white satin petticoat worn at Washington's inauguration ball.

FRANCE BECAME WORLD RENOWNED for luxury fashions such as this green quilted gown of silk damask made in the seventeenth century (opposite and above). Wealthy buyers on the Continent and in the new colonial settlements in the Americas found these garments as irresistible as did the French themselves.

A Passion for Quilted Petticoats

Quilted silk and satin petticoats were à la mode among colonial women of fashion from the beginning to the end of the eighteenth century. Elisabeth McClellan quotes the diary entry of Philip Fithian of Virginia for June 24, 1774, which describes his encounter with Jenny Washington, age seventeen, at a breakfast party: "Her dress is rich and well-chosen, but not tawdry, nor yet too plain. She appears today in a chintz cotton gown with an elegant blue stamp, a sky-blue silk quilt [petticoat], and spotted apron." In Europe too throughout the eighteenth century women wore quilted silk and satin petticoats. These decorative garments usually appeared under split-skirt panels, short jackets, or dressy aprons. Because of their decorative quilting, they had much in common with Provençal *cotillons* (quilted petticoats). They were constructed of lengths of one fabric, white or colored, silk or cotton. Although the upper body was quilted in a simple pattern, usually a diamond grid, the bottom border and sometimes the exposed front panel were embellished with quilted floral, geometric, and occasionally figurative motifs.

Petticoats and other garments quilted in simple motifs had never been unique to Provence. Professional needlewomen in England also stitched quilted articles. A 1563 London broadsheet advertised the services of "Broyderers, Taylors, Quylters and Limners."

BANDS OF WINE AND PALE GREEN in this luscious silk cotillon from about 1780 suggest the color of grapes. Simple quilting in the body is counterbalanced by a border featuring a tessellated diamond grid and floral motifs.

AN EMBROIDERED ENGLISH PILLOW COVER *dated 1715 (opposite) is covered with exotic flowers and bizarre motifs worked in silk and metal thread on a quilted linen base.* FIGURES OF A MAN AND WOMAN, ANIMALS, BIRDS, AND STYLIZED FLOWERS— *as well as an English motto—embellish an American petticoat from 1750 (below).*

Quilted goods were also imported. When the British East India Company opened trade with India in 1600, it gained profitable access to quilted cottons and silks sought for clothing and domestic use in England. In *Trade Goods* Alice Beer cites a letter from two East India Company representatives, Thomas Kerridge and Thomas Rastell, that instructed suppliers at Agra to provide quilts, "some, all of one kind chinte, the lynings and uper parts of one and the same; some of different chintes, yet such as either side may be used. … His Lordship had three or four which he bought lasker [sic] stichte with cullered silke, that will give good contente in England.… " Access to silk goods was critical because England had no significant domestic silk production until the 1680s, according to Rothstein.

It was not the ubiquitous simple quilted petticoat that took fashion's fancy in eighteenth-century Europe and the Americas but rather the decorative quilted petticoat featuring quilted motifs on borders and front panels. This fashion trend followed a period of intense trade activity with Marseilles, where decorative quilted needlework was produced in large quantities for export. Despite having their own domestic and Indian sources of quilted work, Britain and other European countries found Marseilles needlework irresistible. Gaspard Carfeuil's report to the Marseilles chamber of commerce that more than forty thousand articles of *toiles piquées* were produced in Marseille in 1680 for export to England, Hamburg, Holland, Italy, Portugal, and Spain is corroborated by records in the receiving countries. In *Every Day Life in the Massachusetts Bay Colony,* George Dow cites the rates of imports and exports set by the English parliament on June 24, 1660, which included "Quilts, of French making, of Callico, of Sattin or other Silke." (Here the word "quilts" refers to all quilted items, including bedcovers and also petticoats and lengths of quilted yardage.) The Marseilles-made luxury textile articles of fine white *mousseline* embellished with elaborate corded work and the elegant silk *cotillons* quilted in decorative floral motifs were clearly desirable throughout the world of fashion and taste.

European desire for Marseilles-produced needlework continued through years of political discord, intense competition for shipping and trade routes, and the acquisition and control of North American colonies. When Britain established trade barriers to protect its own textile industries and colonial markets from French and other European goods, merchants found means to bend or break the laws to satisfy consumer appetite for fine Marseilles work, even during times of outright war.

AN AMERICAN LINEN PRESS *(pages 106–7) reveals a collection of imported French textiles. The late-eighteenth-century piece holds a child's bodice and several quilted bedcovers of the same era. A white American quilt at right has elegant stuffed trailing motifs in picturesque floral forms similar to broderie de Marseille.*

French Goods and British Traders

Traders from England sought trade with Marseilles in 1613, beginning a commercial relationship that continued for two centuries—legal when relations were calm, illegal during periods of hostility. In 1749, according to Gaston Rambert in the sixth volume of his *Histoire du commerce de Marseille,* 190 British trading ships docked in Marseilles, even though France and Britain were at war that year. Profit was more powerful than patriotism. From 1740 to 1780, years of intense competition and aggression between Britain and France, Marseilles records show that British agents imported great quantities of textiles directly from the Mediterranean port city: lengths of silk (plain, embroidered, and quilted), corded and quilted white cotton, and printed cottons. "It goes without saying," Rambert noted, "that all this contraband cloth sold to the English had to be insinuated as Swiss-made."

The Dutch, as intermediaries, allowed London merchants to obtain Marseilles products through legal means. Amsterdam agents had been major customers for Marseilles needlework since Dutch traders penetrated Mediterranean ports in 1612. The 1783 *Encyclopédie méthodique: Commerce* lists an array of trade goods that the Dutch avidly sought in Marseilles over a long period of time and in great quantities: olive oil, soap, liqueurs, dried figs and raisins, perfumes, and *"des piqueures [sic] de Marseille."* Charles II of England granted special trading privileges—"free ships, free goods"—to Holland in 1667. Under this dispensation Dutch traders could import Marseilles products to Amsterdam, where London merchants could legally purchase them, a happy relationship that lasted until nearly the end of the eighteenth century.

Inventory listings and surviving textiles suggest that these products reached Britain. According to Florence Montgomery in *Textiles in America: 1650–1870,* records from the late 1760s of Hopetoun House in Edinburgh, Scotland, describe a dressing table cover with a skirt of fringed crimson silk falling from a "top covered with Marseils or other fine Quilting made to the Shape." A large bedcover of unknown date found in Edinburgh, submitted to the British Quilters' Guild national indexing project and included in the guild's publication *Quilt Treasures,* is identical in needlework technique and motifs to the early-eighteenth-century work produced in professional Marseilles ateliers and may have come from one of the many workshops there.

Almost all petticoats of the period, whether of French or British origin, were similar, consisting of two long rectangles of cloth with batting held in between by lines of stitching. The top was gathered onto a twill tape to fit the waist. The hem was reinforced by corded edging. Open slits at each side allowed access to pockets tied underneath. All petticoats were stitched with repeated grid or overlapping scale patterns in the upper body and more decorative patterns in the quilted border. The repertoire of design motifs worked in British petticoat borders are noticeably similar to those

LOUIS XV (1715–74) RULED FRANCE when this magnificent gold silk bedcover was stitched and the fishing tableau was painted in the Villa Provençale in Marseilles. British quilters picked up similar motifs for their bedcovers and petticoats, emulating the coronet-topped monogram surrounded by palm fronds, pomegranates, and flowers.

worked in *cotillons:* stylized flowers and garlands; floral vases and urns; fruit forms such as melons, pineapples, pomegranates; and thistles, symbolic images such as hearts, and even human and animal figures.

British ladies recognized the French as fashion leaders and sought French fashion dolls dressed in the latest Paris styles for their dressmakers to copy. In the first half of the eighteenth century, notes McClellan, such dolls were sent monthly from Paris to London. McClellan quotes a satirist in *The Spectator* mocking a London woman's fashion anxiety: "I was almost in despair of ever seeing a model from the dear country, when last Sunday I overheard a lady in the next pew to me whisper to another that at the Seven Stars in King Street, Covent Garden, there was a Mademoiselle completely dressed just come from Paris." This fashion anxiety increased from 1739 to 1783, a time of animosity between Britain and France, and provided a continuing target for the satirist: "You cannot imagine how ridiculously I find we have all been trussed up during the war and how infinitely the French dress excels ours." Clearly, the importation of French dress goods through Dutch intermediaries and illegal commerce was difficult.

When French styles could not be bought directly, they had to be imitated, using whatever materials and needlework techniques were at hand. In "Ready-made Clothing, Guilds, and Women Workers, 1650–1800," Beverly Lemire cites a 1747 British reference to sources of quilted goods: "There have been some ... who

THE FASHION OF REVEALING UNDERWEAR (PETTICOATS) AS OUTERWEAR *originated in the royal courts of France but spread throughout Europe. French Huguenots who fled to England may have designed the fabric for this split-front gown of silk worn over a quilted satin petticoat manufactured in Spitalfields, England, in the mid-1700s.*

used to buy in the Materials wholesale, which they put out to be made in Quilts, and so served the Shops therewith, as they wanted them, by which Trade they got a great deal of Money." Many surviving eighteenth-century quilted English petticoats show construction and design elements similar to those associated with Provence but with slight differences in execution and fabrics that increased over time.

During the latter half of the eighteenth century, when commerce between France and Britain diminished because of mutual hostilities, Marseilles ateliers added articles of stuffed *broderie de Marseille* to their quilting tradition. In Britain, however, there is little evidence of a stuffed-work quilting tradition. Averil Colby in *Quilting* makes little mention of French quilts but notes that American quilted and stuffed all-white bedcovers "have no rivals in English or Welsh quilting." A piece dated 1807 in the British Quilters' Guild survey is assigned a possible provenance of India. Corded and stuffed French quilts probably did not arrive in Britain in quantities to influence the British quilting tradition. Moreover, as Sally Garoutte notes in "Marseilles Quilts and Their Woven Offspring," George Glascow and Robert Elder in 1763 filed a British patent for a "new method of weaving and quilting in the loom, in every method, fashion and figure, as well as in imitations of the common manner of quilting, as of India, French and Marseilles quilting." Thereafter in Britain "Marseilles quilts" were widely recognized as the loom-woven version.

AN IMITATION OF FRENCH WORK, rather than an import from Marseilles, the quilted silk petticoat under this Spitalfields gown of brocaded silk dates to 1743. Although the quilted floral forms emulate the design repertoire of Marseilles ateliers, the stitching technique used to create them and their larger scale reflect an adapted style.

French Luxuries and the Colonists

Quilted garments and bedcovers were colorful elements of fashion and decor in late-seventeenth-century New England, just as they were in England. Hundreds of bed quilts and petticoats are listed in the estate inventory records in Suffolk County, Probate Court of the Massachusetts Bay Colony, for the period 1689–1703. The 1693 inventory of Thomas Pemberton, for example, lists one "red silk quilt for a bed." The 1695 inventory of the estate of Jane Phelps lists a white silk petticoat with silver lace, "1 Orange-colour Cloth petticoat of Silver," one silk counterpane, two red petticoats trimmed in gold and silver lace, and a quilted silk waistcoat. These textiles could have come through London, as British East India Company imports from India, or could have originated in Marseilles. A red silk quilt lined with yellow silk listed in the 1698 inventory of John Bankes reflects a color combination common to Provence and suggests a possible Marseilles origin.

Rejecting expected allegiance to the mother country, New England colonists attempted independent trade with other European ports. In 1642 ships sailed from Boston to France and Spain to trade raw wool from the colonies for wines, fruits, and other luxury goods, according to Dow. The English parliament, distraught at losing its monopoly on colonial goods and markets, took stern protective action. In 1645 England's first Navigation Acts disallowed commerce between colonies in New England and other European countries. In reality, during the 150 years the acts were in place an enormous amount of evasive commerce and blatant smuggling in textiles and other goods occurred. Dow quotes the complaint of the Boston merchant Edward Randolph in 1676: "They trade with most parts of Europe from which they import direct all kinds of merchandise, so that little is left for English merchants to import."

In bold defiance of the Navigation Acts, ship captains from New England ports opened trade with Marseilles. Depositions penned by Marseilles notaries recorded that Boston captains John Colter and "Th." Baillie arrived on the *Marka* and the *Gervefood* in 1735. Two British captains sailed to Marseilles from Philadelphia in 1739. Captain George Davis anchored *l'Industrie* on February 19 and Captain Guillaume Wallace *le Nancey* on March 10. (The odd spellings make sense in French, but even the French authors of the *Histoire du commerce de Marseille* had trouble reading records of notaries whose first language was Provençal: "The names of ships and even the ports of origin declared by the captains are often barely decipherable as the scribes are as little as possible familiar with

English. So that the second of April, the [American] vessel *Priscellia* [sic] is declared as the *Piscadoue,* a consonance more Provençal than English.")

French styles in fashion and interior decor were desired by colonists as much as by Londoners. Access to French goods was available legally through London merchants who had contacts with Dutch intermediaries and illegally from ships of all flags, including colonists', that braved English blockades. Colonists could also satisfy their taste for French goods by a third route. In the 1660s, despite the Navigation Acts, New England ships began commerce with the French Caribbean colony of Martinique. Privateers along the Atlantic coast maintained illegal supply routes to the

extent that the governor of the Massachusetts Bay Colony, Simon Bradstreet, complained in 1690 of the damage "French Privateers and Pirates" were wreaking on legal shipping, according to Dow. Charleston, South Carolina, had an active trade with French Caribbean merchants as well, based on its residents' fascination with all things French.

As Susan Burrows Swan notes in *Plain and Fancy: American Women and Their Needlework, 1700–1850,* "French was another eighteenth-century subject that enhanced the image of accomplished ladies. Charleston schools offered it as early as 1739; because the city conducted important trade with the French West Indies, men learned French to expedite their business. Young

ELEGANT COUTURE EXPORTED TO THE CREOLES in the French-Caribbean islands included items such as this silk damask caraco, stiffened with stays, and a yellow silk taffeta jupon in broderie de Marseille, woven in Avignon. Waiting Creole women reportedly bought all but two pieces of a 1704 French shipment of worked silks.

ladies learned it to expedite their business of attracting men." This trade with the French West Indies was the route by which significant amounts of Marseilles-originated needlework arrived in the American colonies. Certainly, Marseilles needlework ended up in great quantities on Martinique, Guadeloupe, and the other French Caribbean islands.

Colonists and Creoles—French citizens born in the French-American colonies of Martinique and Guadeloupe—desired all the luxury products of their mother country. As French citizens in informal colonial exile, they clung to their culture and aristocratic tastes. Even Napoléon Bonaparte's first wife, Joséphine, was born in Martinique on June 23, 1763. Proceeds from enormous indigo, cocoa, and sugar plantations easily covered costs of expensive imports.

Captain Nicolas Arnoul's 1670 expedition to Martinique, laden with *toiles de Marseille,* launched a trade satisfying to both Marseilles merchants and consumers in "les Iles" (the French colonies in the Caribbean), according to Rambert. Within a few years the Marseilles entrepreneur Joseph Fabre established the Compagnie de la Mediterranée to satisfy Creole demand for printed *indiennes* and lengths of plain and quilted colored silks worked in motifs of bouquets or fields of flowers. Three cases of corded and embroidered Marseilles cloth shipped to the West Indies in 1695 were received with a "veritable passion" by the Creole women, Fabre wrote in his memoirs. Another Marseilles merchant, P. Labat, wrote of a 1704 shipment of Marseilles textiles that sold as soon as the bundles were open: " … as for payment the island women … brought sugar cane, indigo and cocoa by moonlight, products the women had their faithful slaves pilfer from storehouses after dark, which they sold to pay for the purchases without knowledge of their husbands and fathers."

By 1719 Martinique imported all Marseilles garment and needlework products: slippers and hats; lengths of plain, printed, embroidered, and quilted fabric; and articles of clothing. By the mid-eighteenth century other businesses specialized in producing clothes: camisoles and chamber robes in *broderie de Marseille,* as well as *casaquins* (short jackets worn by women) and more chamber robes made from *indiennes.* Ateliers that specialized in finely stitched bed furnishings for export to "les Iles" had "grown considerably" by 1771, according to Georges Grosson's *Almanach historique de Marseille.* Three *tapissiers* who specialized in production of *broderie de Marseille* needlework bedcovers for export to "les Iles" are listed in the 1789 edition of the *Guide Mazet,* a Marseilles business directory, along with addresses:

Daumas, Louis Md Tapissier faisant pour les Isles tous sortes de Meubles, rue Paradis

Michel, Fr Tapissier faisant pour les Isles toute sorte de meubles relativement aux usages du Pays, rue St.-Ferréol

Soutete, Fr Md d'Etoffes de toutes couleurs & meubles pour les Isles relatifs aux usages du Pays, rue St.-Ferréol

GEOMETRIC ZIGZAG LINE AND STAR PATTERNS enliven a chamber robe of pale green sateen cotton (opposite). Similar to others found in Marseilles, it is believed to have been made in Moroccan workshops in imitation of Marseilles needlework. It lies on an eighteenth-century quilted bedcover of cotton printed with lush swags of wisteria.

Smuggled Goods or Flattering Imitations?

The *tapissier* ateliers of Marseilles produced prolifically for export, often reproducing successful designs many times over, particularly in wedding quilts. Several examples of Marseilles needlework have been found in the United States, suggesting that importation routes, legal or not, existed. One exquisitely corded and stuffed wedding quilt made around 1800 and found in Paris is identical to two others, one in the Musée de Vieux Marseille and one found in Massachusetts. Another *broderie de Marseille* wedding quilt dated about 1790 was uncovered in a priest's trunk when it was sold at auction in Illinois in 1960. Other pieces made in the distinct Marseilles style exist in various museums throughout the United States.

It is difficult to assess the amount of French needlework that actually arrived in the thirteen American colonies because contraband was not likely to be reported in official documents. However, other records show that by the early 1700s French quilted work enjoyed wide repute. In the March 2, 1712, edition of the *Boston Newsletter,* George Brownell, a sewing instructor, advertised lessons in English and French quilting "embroideri [sic] and flourishings." Presumably the lessons taught either corded *broderie de Marseille* or simple quilting techniques at this time, as stuffed *broderie de Marseille* did not play a significant role in the Provençal quilting tradition until fifty years later.

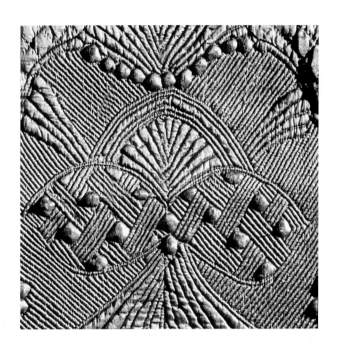

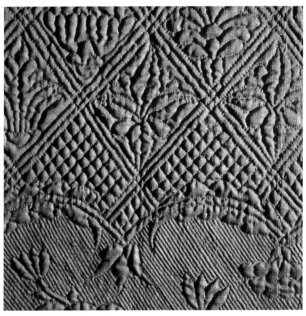

THE PROVENANCE OF VARIOUS QUILTS remains a mystery. A blue silk petticoat (top) from 1770–75 was "sent from London," according to family notes, but its motifs and needlework suggest a Marseilles origin. A red glazed-wool petticoat (bottom) with a decorative border is probably an English or colonial needleworker's emulation of French quilting.

The French influence on colonial fashion extended to adoption of new words. The French word *cotillon* can be traced to 1461. By the end of the seventeenth century the meaning expanded from a quilted petticoat to refer to a festive dance as well as the dressy attire worn to such an event. American Southerners to this day know a cotillion as a society event with dancing, where debutantes are presented in formal finery.

Two citations refer to textiles that apparently came from London, although they are described as "Marseilles" and "Marcels." According to Mildred B. Lanier in "Marseilles Quiltings of the Eighteenth and Nineteenth Centuries," on August 5, 1739, Henry Purefoy wrote to the London merchant Anthony Baxter about an imported Marseilles petticoat, "I received all the things in the box and have returned to you the Marseilles Quilt petticoat by Mr. Eagles, the carrier. It is so heavy my mother cannot wearing [sic] it." Florence Montgomery in *Textiles in America: 1650–1870* writes that the "Marcels bed and canopy—cost 20 guineas" owned by Eliza Pinckney of Charleston, South Carolina, about 1745, was imported via Britain. A third citation with no mention of geographic origin, also by Lanier, is a 1756 reference to "40 yards of French quilting," found in records from Frederick Hall, a Virginia plantation. Whether these three items originated in Marseilles and were shipped via Amsterdam, were transported as contraband, or were British imitations of Marseilles quilting does not contradict the notion that French needlework had an influence on British and American decorative textiles—if only in name.

Some quilted petticoats and bedcovers surviving in the United States have decorative motifs worked in techniques identical to Marseilles needlework. It is frustrating not to know their exact provenance. Other eighteenth-century American quilts are much like Marseilles products in basic form and design; however, they are constructed of materials not typical of French pieces, and their patterns are worked in an enlarged scale and with a flatter surface relief. The difficulty and expense of obtaining contraband textiles apparently prompted imitation of French quilted needlework in the British colonies as in Britain.

Many American quilted petticoats and bedcovers, constructed and embellished like Marseilles work, were made of glazed wool and filled with woolen batting, materials rarely used in Provençal *cotillons* and bedcovers and never mentioned in export records. Yet American quilted motifs were strikingly similar to those on work from Provence and can be compared with motifs seen on French and American needlework.

Any notion that the American tradition of stuffed quilted work originated in Britain is not borne out by evidence. Few surviving examples of British stuffed-work quilts exist, nor does firm documentation that it was commonly practiced there. Such quilts that do exist have an uncertain provenance. The American stuffed-work tradition may have been wholly influenced by French models, imported through the French West Indies.

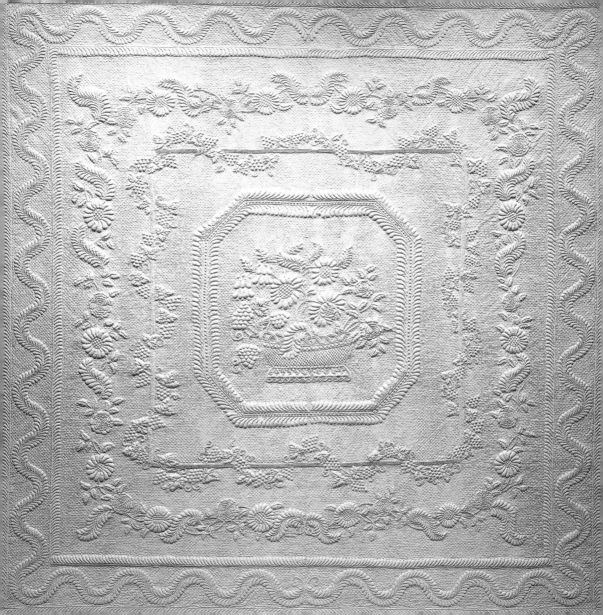

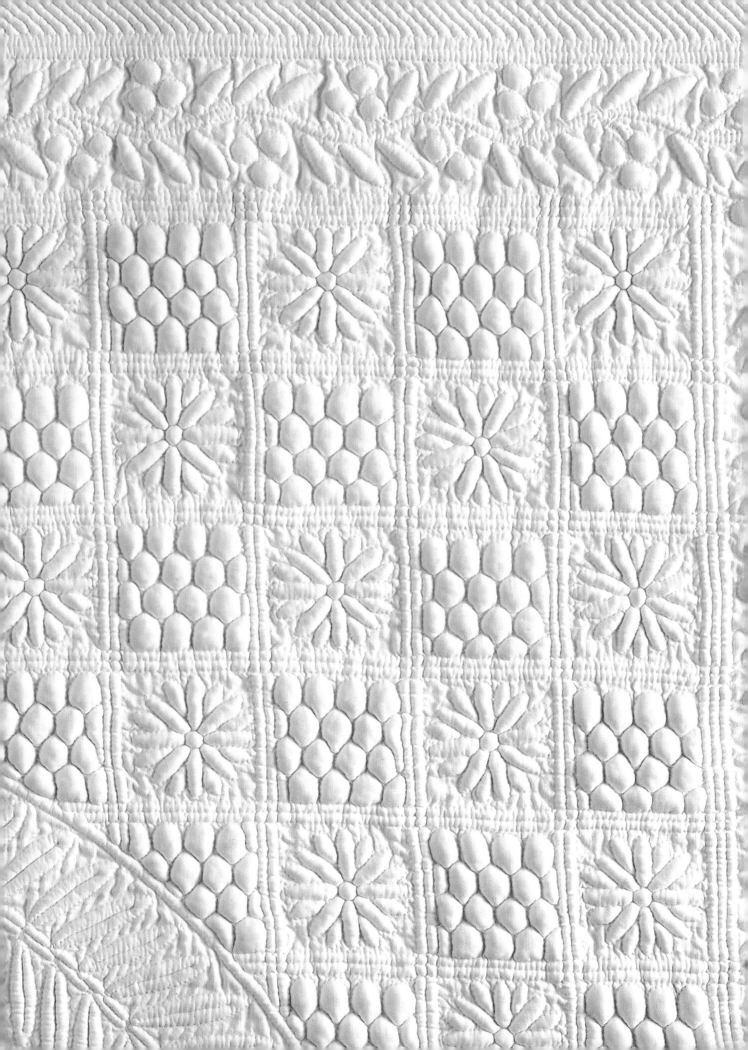

The French Connection

If technique, construction, and design are so similar among French, British, and American quilted needlework and if these works were all made within a relatively short time span, why theorize that French needlework influenced British and American needlework? A compelling argument is that only Provence had a long tradition of quilted needlework that dated to the Middle Ages, was highly sophisticated by the fifteenth century, and was distributed widely in the seventeenth century. No other region in Europe had a long-standing quilting tradition coupled with high levels of export activity. Even the ateliers in Sicily and Naples do not seem to have produced significant amounts of corded, stuffed, and quilted work after it appeared at the end of the fourteenth century; in fact, Italians were among the chief importers of *broderie de Marseille.* Quilted works from India were apparently widely exported, but surviving examples attributed as Indo-Portuguese are not as refined in workmanship as Marseilles products, and India never held the position of fashion leader as did France. The extraordinarily high export levels of Marseilles needlework recorded in 1680 gave opportunity for exposure throughout Europe and potential influence on other needlework traditions.

Specifically, design vestiges of *broderie de Marseille* appeared in British and American quilted petticoats, even though actual cording was infrequently used

*A SEA GREEN SATIN PETTICOAT found in America and attributed as an English import
of 1740–50 (top and bottom) simulates broderie de Marseille designs: puffed diamond
and floral forms, curvaceous leaf fronds, and closely set parallel-line stitching. In construction,
dimensions, and motifs, it is strikingly similar to the petticoat shown on page 117 (top).*

in them. Almost all quilting design forms in surviving British and American petticoat borders show ghosts of patterns that had been achieved with cording in their French counterparts. These include the prevalence of parallel diagonal lines stitched as a ground for other decorative motifs, rows of parallel stitching on the border of a bedcover or petticoat, similar in appearance to the actual corded edging traditional to Marseilles needlework, and the frequent use of diamond puffed grids.

American women did stitch corded, stuffed, and quilted bedcovers, although not with a completely filled ground of cording. When corded work was practiced by colonial needlewomen, it frequently was associated with French work. In the December 25–January 1, 1750, issue of the *South Carolina Gazette*, Mary and John Irwin, owners of a French school in Charleston, advertised classes that "draw from Marseille [sic] quilting and all sorts of embroidery." John Paul Grimke, a jeweler, advertised "imported Marsella bodkins and needles" in the November 10–17, 1759, issue of the *Gazette*.

After the American Revolution the love affair between France and the new United States of America gained in ardor, but commercial activity dropped. Rambert states that the falloff in trade was a result not of lack of American desire for French goods but of Marseilles merchants not being paid by Americans, who had not yet covered their war debts. Thomas Jefferson, the new ambassador to France, attempted to redress the trade imbalance by visiting Marseilles to promote American products among port entrepreneurs several months before the French Revolution. The civil uprising in France ended Jefferson's efforts in Marseilles, and exports of Marseilles products to the new American republic, including needlework, stopped.

Needlework production and export to the French-Caribbean colonies continued through the French Revolution but dwindled with the establishment of the First Empire in 1804. Citizens of the new French Republic understandably scorned the trappings of aristocracy, and the centuries-long fascination with quilted petticoats ended abruptly. The beautiful young Empress Joséphine adopted the new, high-waisted silhouette of the French Republic and made body-clinging gowns of sheer, light cottons fashionable around the world. The international blockades during the Napoleonic Wars, beginning in 1807, effectively isolated France, Britain, and the United States from one another. Such isolation could explain why techniques and motifs in British and American whole-cloth quilted bedcovers began to differ radically from French models. (Quilted petticoats dropped from fashion at the end of the eighteenth century.)

By about 1700 British needlewomen were pursuing the creative possibilities of pieced-work quilts. Only in Wales and the North Country did quilters adopt a bedcover tradition of whole-cloth and "strippy" quilts (made up of alternate bars of complementary fabrics). However, both whole-cloth and strippy bedcovers were quilted in medallion or all-over

PROVENÇAL WOMEN IN THE EARLY NINETEENTH CENTURY retained affection for quilted silk cotillons, paired at left here with a short caraco jacket and a printed cotton fichu. Yet fashionable Parisiennes of the Empire era (1804–14) might appear in a slim dress of sheer mousseline draped with a shawl of kashmir cones.

compositions that incorporated motifs of local significance outside the French repertoire.

American quilters continued to produce all-white quilted wonders, occasionally corded and stuffed, although design motifs were more widely spaced and not as high as those associated with *broderie de Marseille*. They too designed their own patterns, incorporating patriotic symbols and images particular to personal interests. Nineteenth-century American needlewomen were devoted to exploring pieced-work and appliqué quilts, two traditions that French needlewomen did not regularly take up until the mid-twentieth century.

One cannot state definitively that *broderie de Marseille* was imported in great volume into Britain or the American colonies; documentation is too scanty. However, evidence does suggest that enough Marseilles needlework arrived in Britain and the American colonies to influence their quilting traditions. The British Navigation Acts did not block distribution, which continued legally via Holland and illegally through scofflaw ship captains—British and American—who even docked in Marseilles and acquired contraband textiles through the French West Indies. The English and American taste for French goods, the many references to Marseilles textiles in English and American records, and the comparison of surviving quilted articles in all three countries allow the possibility of direct—and the probability of at least indirect—influence of *broderie de Marseille* on quilted, corded, and stuffed textiles stitched in Britain and America.

AMERICANS TURNED THEIR ATTENTION TO PIECED QUILTS, *but one from about 1830 still reached for the French touch—incorporating decidedly French fabrics in its rainbow checkerboard maze.*

Continuing the Tradition

TYPICAL PROVENÇAL FINERY *in the nineteenth century combined lively prints and colors.*
At left a printed cotton gown dating to about 1880 is worn over a quilted lightweight
wool petticoat in brilliant violet. At right a blue apron sets off a midcentury collection
of printed cottons fashioned into a fichu, caraco, and quilted jupon.

OR THE CHRISTENING OF AN INFANT *in nineteenth-century Provence, the baby was often tucked into a small, all-white quilted cotton petassoun, which was stitched and corded in delightful decorative motifs. Cradled in such pretty work, the baby was introduced to the social world as a treasured little being. When accidents occurred, the cleaning power of renowned Marseilles soap together with exposure to the strong Provençal sunlight removed stains and restored the piece to pristine whiteness.*

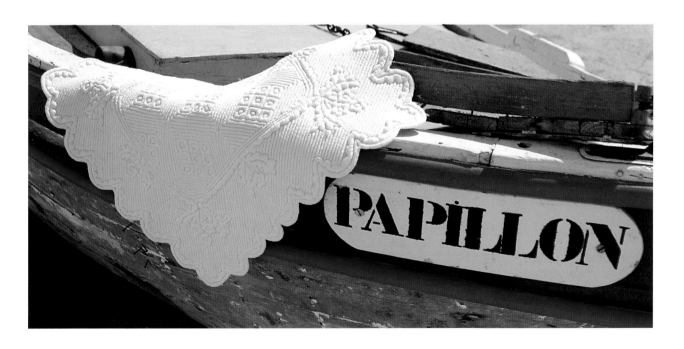

LAUREL LEAVES AND WAVE FORMS make up the border of a nineteenth-century cotton bedcover (opposite), which was worked in a tile-patterned grid.
TO PROTECT MOTHERS' ATTIRE FROM DRIPS AND DRIBBLES, women from fishing villages such as La Ciotat made exquisite infant petassouns (above) for sale in the late 1800s.

Les Boutis

Boutis is a nineteenth-century Provençal word with broad definition. Provençal women used it to refer to the corded or quilted needlework technique for making *jupons* (petticoats), *couvre-lits* (large bedcovers), *vannes* or *vanhos* (small bedcovers), and *petassouns* (infant pieces). *Boutis* was also the term given to the blunt-nosed needle used to draw cording through narrow channels of stitching. The Provençal-French dictionary published by the Provençal poet Frédéric Mistral in 1886, *Lou tresor doù felibrige ou dictionnaire provençal-français,* conforms with oral tradition by defining *boutis* as *"piqué de Marseille"* work and as white needlework that was stitched by the young women of two fishing villages near Marseilles, Cassis and La Ciotat, known for their sardine harvests. However, the Provençal word apparently never passed into common French usage. The eleven-volume *Grand Robert: Dictionnaire de la langue française* does not mention needlework in its definition of *boutis.* Rather, it defines *boutis* as the furrow in the ground made by the snout of a wild boar in search of truffles and edible roots. So much for respect for women's work.

During the nineteenth century young women from the Mediterranean fishing villages produced

petassouns to sell to fine families of the area. Frédéric Mistral celebrated their needle skills in his epic poem *Calendau:*

> Others stitch the fine cloth,
> to make le boutis, divine work
> that resembles a meadow, when the frost
> embroiders all in white each leaf and stem.

Calendau (1867), Chant III, lines 402–5

Mistral's lovely imagery is borne out by the delicate designs of pieces made in these fishing villages. Harmonious compositions featured a central figure, such as an intricate, puffed, diamond grid pattern or a floral medallion surrounded by trailing leaves and garlands. Other motifs—floral sprays, small acorns or grapes on the vine, decorated corners and side borders—symbolized good fortune and prosperity for the new baby. All figures rested on a bed of diagonal corded lines that made the work supple and absorbent. Most *petassouns* had scalloped borders embellished with inner corded scallops.

To make *petassouns* village needlewomen revived the technique of corded *broderie de Marseille,* working designs in a slightly larger scale and using cording of larger diameter than in the previous century. The pieces were quite small, no larger than twenty inches square. Following the steps involved in *broderie de Marseille,*

THE POET FRÉDÉRIC MISTRAL (1830–1914) sought to revitalize Provençal culture through his work long before it was fashionable to seek one's roots. With money from his 1904 Nobel Prize—for "Mireio," his epic poem about his native Provence—he established the Museon Arlaten, which celebrates Provençal culture.

*QUILTING MOTIFS FOR PETASSOUNS varied from plain pieces quilted
in a diamond grid with a corded edge (below) to finely articulated floral
and herbal compositions and broderie de Marseille corded work.*

needlewomen used a template to trace a pattern on the top layer of fine white cotton percale and then stitched parallel lines or small compartments as the pattern dictated, using tiny running stitches. When all the motifs were stitched, they drew cording through the channels to raise surface contours and effect a play of light and shadow that revealed pattern. Small circles of cording, not batting, filled pattern compartments to form flower centers and other small rounded design elements.

No one knows how or when this cottage industry began. Little else in the lives of these women in seacoast villages reflected refinement, and other, more crude needlework was pressing, as Mistral depicted in his poem:

> *We had the evening: my mother,*
> *with the thread she spun by hand,*
> *repaired the torn sails;*
> *We the children repaired the nets,*
> *pulled, pushed the needle,*
> *first over, then under*
> *we mended the torn meshes of the nets*
> *that hung by a nail on the wall.*

Chant IV, lines 36–42

The distinct design repertoire executed in *broderie de Marseille* makes the *petassouns* from fishing villages immediately recognizable. Other Provençal needlewomen, working at home or for local households, made ceremonial and practical *petassouns* as well, using a range of techniques and fabrics.

*MOST ALL-WHITE PETASSOUNS, although of washable cotton, were decorative—
clearly intended for christenings and other special social occasions (pages 134–35).
Other infant pieces were assembled more hastily of various cotton printed fabrics
and appear to have been made for everyday use with the baby.*

The Flourishing of Folk Art

Regional use of the word *boutis* reflected the limited distribution of nineteenth-century Provençal handwork. The international market for Marseilles needlework that prevailed during the seventeenth and eighteenth centuries no longer existed. Professional needlewomen produced work not for export but for local households. Most quilting in this period was by individuals for their own use. It was cruder than work accomplished by professionals for a world market; women working at home with many other duties had little time for fine stitchery. Because they were creating things they wanted to have around them rather than making goods to order, any loss of refinement was eclipsed by a spontaneity and exuberance in their work. Domestic needlewomen infused the refined tradition of corded, stuffed, and quilted needle arts with new creative elements, some brought about by necessity and some by the happy consequences that result whenever an art is adapted by a larger population.

During the nineteenth century textiles were available and affordable as never before. Markets and shops were full of silks and cottons in a rainbow of hues, assorted weaves, and varied cotton prints. From this abundance women selected fabrics and created quilted goods that reflected their individual ideals of

THE NINETEENTH CENTURY WITNESSED A GREAT CHANGE *in the look of Provençal quilting, but the result was as distinctive in its own way as the work formerly done in professional ateliers. Arabesque, floral, and toile de Jouy patterns, popular in France throughout the century, appeared in quilted French bedcovers of this period.*

beauty. Above all, they took the notion of quilting as a sculptural, three-dimensional art form and exaggerated it, raising it to new heights. Motifs that had been heightened by precisely worked channels filled with slim cording and tiny compartments lined with bits of stuffing were enlarged and amplified. Instead of miniature gardens, Provençal women stitched lush bowers of fruits and flowers; hearts swelled up in soft curves, and geometric forms such as diamonds and squares billowed above the straight lines of stitching that shaped them. Nineteenth-century Provençal quilted petticoats and bedcovers were amply embellished with forms executed in robust, large-scale relief.

The quilting technique was standard: batting was sandwiched between two layers of fabric, while lines of stitching worked in various decorative patterns held together all the layers. Fairly thick batting ensured a high, padded surface relief. Large stitches sufficed to delineate pattern; the materials were too thick for delicate work. The quilter maintained a firm tension on her thread as she stitched, so that the lines of stitching would recede between batting-filled pattern areas. The more meticulous quilter separated wads of batting into pattern compartments as she worked, so that the top and bottom fabrics almost touched each other along stitching lines; as a result, surface contours were even more pronounced.

THREE SILK BOURRETTE WEAVES, piecced together and backed with printed cotton,
were selected to create a vibrantly colored, early-nineteenth-century bedcover (above).
A DRAPERY SWAG AND TASSEL QUILTING MOTIF was used for a Provençal bedcover made
of a variegated, serpentine-print cotton dating from about 1850 (pages 138–39).

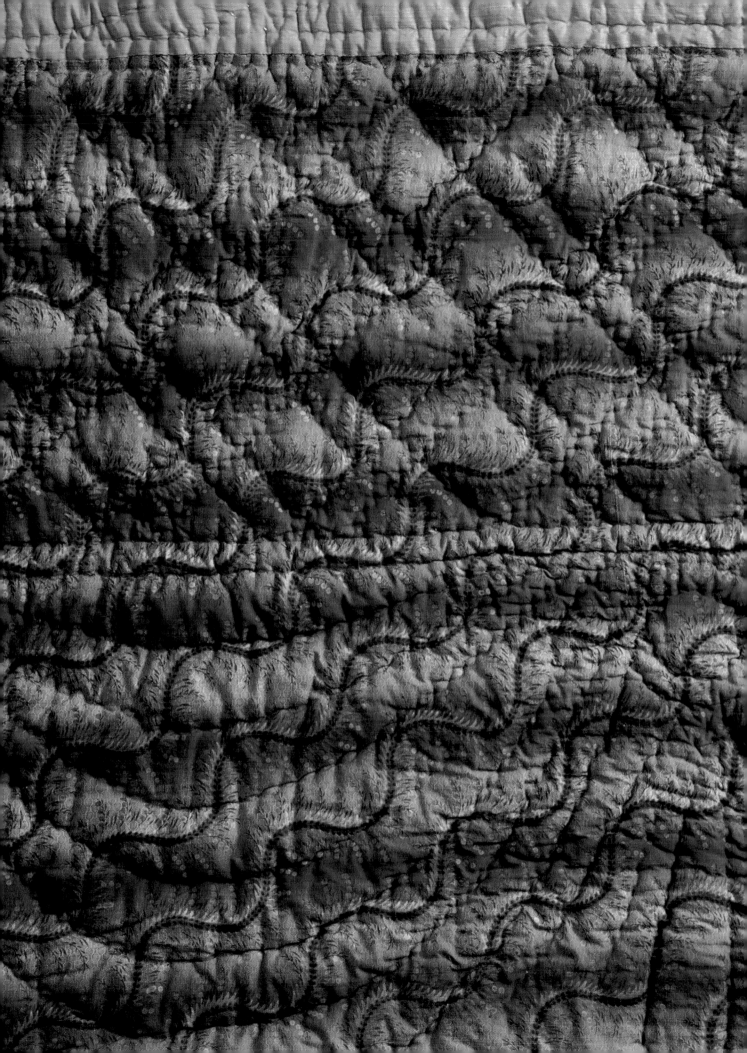

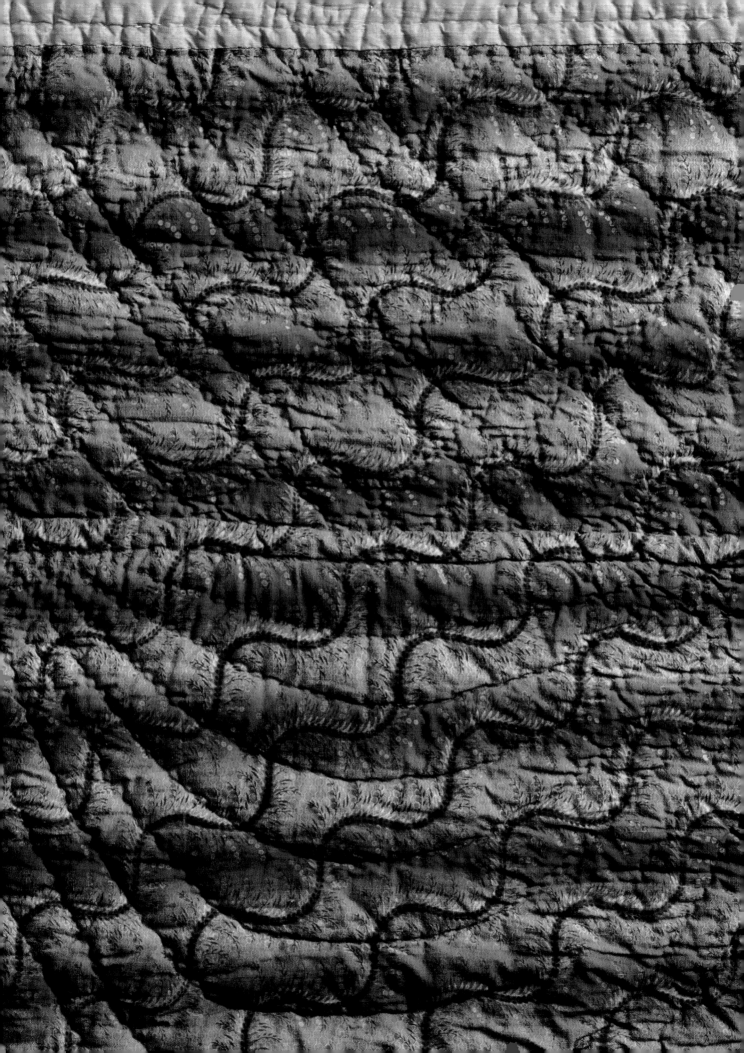

Celebrating Provençal Life

Provençal quilters, making things for their own pleasure and use, drew ideas from old patterns and added their own motifs of regional significance. Many patterns can be loosely identified with periods of fashion driven by changes in government. During the First Empire (1804–14) needlewomen favored laurel garlands, puffed diamonds, and floral figures organized within geometric lines. The Restoration (1814–48) witnessed a renaissance of curved scrolls, cornucopias, and flower-filled baskets, vases, and urns. The design repertoire of the Second Empire (1851–70) held an abundance of fertile fruit and flower forms strewn in lush disorder. Throughout the century these patterns were mingled with representations of Provençal melons, grapes, French *coqs* and *fleur-de-lys,* love birds, indigenous flowers and fruits, the dove of the Holy Spirit (if the quilter was Protestant), occasional initials and dates, and always hearts—tucked in corners, doubled and lapped one over another, pierced with arrows, and borne by cupids.

Remarkably, although cording was no longer used, vestiges of the straight-line design forms previously created by cording can be seen in close-set parallel lines of stitching through thick batting. These lines appear as framing elements and are always seen on edges. Almost without exception quilted bedcovers and quilted *jupons* are finished at

A FOREST GREEN GLAZED COTTON BEDCOVER, made about 1840, is backed with a green-and-yellow check. The glazed terra-cotta jardiniers, olive oil jar, and wine jugs typify nineteenth-century pots from southern France.

the edge with at least two but more commonly multiple rows of parallel stitching lines.

Provençal women never explored patchwork or pieced work, the rather contrary notion of cutting cloth into tiny pieces only to reassemble them into fanciful geometric shapes, as British and American women did. Occasional examples of pieced work are found in France and Provence, such as mosaics pieced of hexagons and triangles cut from whimsical prints, but these rarely show an orderly arrangement of colors or shapes. The pieced-work *jupon* worn by the fish vendor in *Arrivée des pêcheurs au quai St.-Jean,* for example, appears to be a thrifty assemblage of usable scraps of fabric, arranged haphazardly. Other exam-

ples of Provençal pieced work dazzle the eye with their striking juxtaposition of prints but do not reveal any intricate composition.

The *fenêtre* (window) composition used for *vannes* (small bedcovers) is the most complicated pieced-textile form traditional to Provence and is found in inventories as early as the sixteenth century. In the *fenêtre* composition the central textile is framed by a wide border of contrasting fabric. When the center was a printed cloth, the center quilting was simple and the border was commonly made of a plain cloth quilted in fanciful forms. *Fenêtre* bedcovers were small, decorative pieces made to rest just on top of the bed, over other covers that served for warmth.

*"ARRIVÉE DES PÊCHEURS AU QUI ST.-JEAN" (1884) by Marius Guindon shows
a group of fish vendors gossiping while they await incoming boats at the Marseilles
docks. The seated woman in the center wears a quilted indienne jupon, while the
one at right wears a jupon pieced from many large, irregularly shaped textile scraps.*

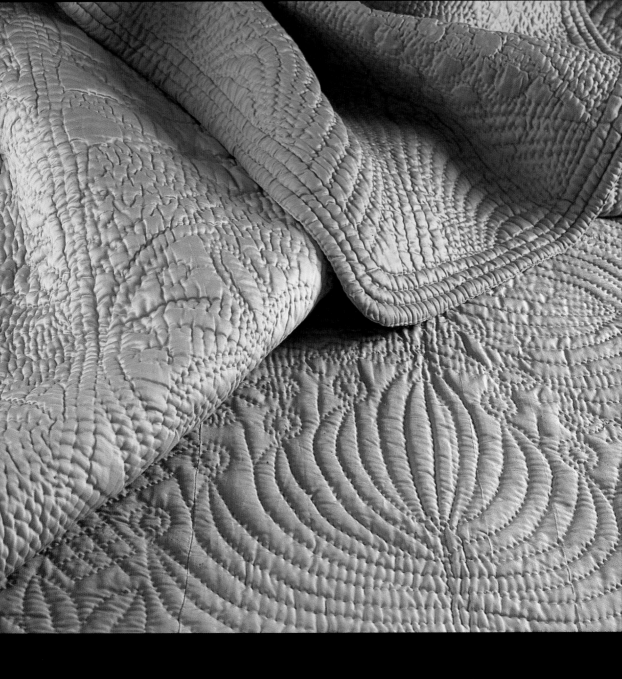

THE PROVENÇAL PALETTE AND IMAGES *are reflected in these two quilted bedcovers.*
The top bedcover, made of two colors of cotton sateen—peach and gold—holds
elaborate floral forms and includes a drapery swag motif in the border. The bottom
bedcover, made of pale lavender silk, features large palm frond motifs.

Art of the Provençal Bedroom

Quilted *couvre-lits* and *vannes* in charming prints and color combinations with sumptuous, high-relief quilting in delightful motifs were prevalent in Provençal homes. Each one was unique, reflecting the maker's taste and skill. When quilts were fashioned of fanciful prints, the quilting was usually uncomplicated, because the decorative effect was provided by the printed pattern. The reverse side of printed bed quilts was often a completely different but complementary printed or plain-colored fabric. When the top fabric of a bedcover was a plain-colored cloth, the quilting was usually highly decorative. None of these rules was fast, and many variations on these themes can be found: quilts made of printed fabrics further embellished with elaborate quilting as well as plain fabrics simply quilted. Provençal needlewomen were adept at combining colors, fabrics, and needlework for attractive results. Nowhere was that skill more evident than in nineteenth-century wedding quilts.

It was Provençal tradition in the nineteenth century, as it had been for the previous two hundred years, to make or to have a local professional make a quilt to be placed on top of the wedding bed. Sometimes made of plain-colored cloth but after mid-century most often made all in white, the quilt was covered in quilted motifs representing femininity, purity, fertility, love, and fidelity, as well as motifs of personal significance such as initials. Surviving pieces are exceedingly appealing to modern eyes, despite crude needlework, because of the charm of the quilted figures. Often the central motif would be a vase of flowers, perhaps marguerites or daisies to symbolize femininity or lilies to symbolize virginity, surrounded by images of abundance and fertility: melons, pomegranates, and bunches of ripe grapes. Wedding quilts made their formal appearance the night of the marriage, on top of the nuptial bed.

Quilted *vannes* were so much a part of local tradition that they entered the Provençal language as idioms and were featured during festival days. The phrase *i'an fa lou lième la vano* translates roughly as "they have made their bed with a bedcover" and refers to newlyweds who abided by social standards and married before having intimate relations. *Faire vano* literally translates as "to go to another bedcover" and figuratively means to leave the family home for another. On festival and saints' days in some towns

DURING THE FRENCH REVOLUTION, *when aristocrats' possessions were destroyed, many luxury textiles were lost. Afterward they were at risk of government confiscation. A notice (above), posted in 1794, ordered citizens of Marseilles to contribute 1,200 bedcovers and 1,200 pairs of bed linens to the Army of the Republic.*

145

women draped their white wedding quilts out of windows and hung them on exterior walls for street decoration. On July 22 women in Saint-Maximum-la- Sainte-Baume used to honor Saint Madeleine by decorating their village with quilted bedcovers of all colors and pretty prints hung from the windows of buildings and houses. Historically in Tarascon during the annual procession of the Tarasque, a vile beast known to gobble up naughty children, mothers waved their white quilts from house windows to frighten away the monster.

In the nineteenth century many all-white *vannes*, presumably used for wedding quilts, were restyled from eighteenth-century quilted petticoats. Few luxury textiles survived the ravages of the French Revolution and the ensuing periods of disruption. Economic hardships may have made it difficult to buy new cloth. A family heirloom in the form of an elaborately corded and quilted petticoat could have held special significance as a wedding quilt. Whatever the reason, many *jupons* were recycled (a word the French frequently used for this practice) by thrifty Provençals. One simply undid the main petticoat seam, cut the long length into equal halves, and sewed together the tops. To finish, the slits that had been made for pockets were stitched up and the edges were bound. Easily a quarter of remaining all-white corded and quilted bedcovers were restyled from pre–French Revolution quilted *jupons*, allowing their fine needlework and textiles to be appreciated in another form.

THE BELLE ÉPOQUE'S FANCY FOR EXOTIC FLORAL PRINTS is seen in two quilted bedcovers from the late nineteenth century (top). A FLORAL RAMONEUR PRINT from about 1790, backed with a blue check, originally served as a quilted jupon (bottom). At some point in the nineteenth century the petticoat was taken apart and restyled into a bedcover.

Jupons and Cotillons

In the nineteenth century the *élégantes* of Paris and the rest of the fashion world may have abandoned quilted silk petticoats, but quilted dress survived in Provence until World War I. The basic item of quilted wear was the pretty printed cotton *jupon* or *cotillon* worn daily by women of modest means in cities and villages. On festival days and Sunday afternoons more fanciful *jupons* appeared for the weekly promenade and social gathering in the town square. These *jupons,* saved for "best," were made of cotton or silk. The *jupon's* elaborate border, quilted in motifs of hearts, cables, leafy boughs, or whatever the wearer thought appropriate and lay within her needle skills, peeped out beneath the hem of her short dress and above layers of under petticoats.

TYPE MARSEILLAIS - POISSONNIÈRE
Y sont pas frais mes Poissons
Vous sias pas regardado Carùturo... An coumo voùs, alors

The quilted *jupon* or *cotillon,* known as *coutihoun* in Provençal, was also integrated into language idioms. If a woman were to *faire un acro a soun coutihoun,* which translates literally as "snare her skirt," she would be having an illicit romance. A *coutihounet* or a *petit jupon* referred to a child who always clung to her mother's skirts.

Until the mid-nineteenth century the wedding *jupon,* made by a dressmaker or the bride herself, was fashioned of silk or cotton in any print or single color—red, yellow, brown, the fashionable and iridescent *gorge de pigeon,* or green, the color that symbolized a young woman's transition from mademoiselle to madame. The fashion for all-white wedding garb as a symbol of chastity did not take hold in Provence until the 1840s. (Joséphine Bonaparte elevated the fashion for virginal, all-white bridal wear when she wore a gown made of sheer white *mousseline* for her marriage to Napoléon in 1796—ironically, her second marriage.)

The borders of a bride's wedding *jupon* held the most fanciful quilting of any in her wardrobe, and a heart was almost certain to be found within the border tableaus. Many wedding petticoats of the period show identical scrolls, flowers, and other motifs because young women commonly exchanged patterns with one another. According to popular belief, a young Provençal woman spent years preparing her trousseau, in particular stitching the *jupons* she would wear as a wife and working her most experienced stitches in her wedding *jupon.*

TEXTILE PRINTERS IN AND AROUND MULHOUSE *produced thousands
of printed cottons with yellow, blue, white, and black flowers and kashmir cones
in the nineteenth century. Jupons fashioned from fabrics made about 1860
were quilted in a diamond grid with corded lines on the border (below).*

*A COSTUME FOR A NINETEENTH-CENTURY PROVENÇAL BRIDE (opposite) featured
an embroidered fichu of pure white mousseline and a gown and apron of brown silk,
tucked up to reveal a quilted white petticoat worked in broderie de Marseille.*

Fashion and Fancy
in the Twentieth Century

The Provençal needlework tradition seems to have diminished greatly as the twentieth century approached. This decline is hard to document in numbers, because quilting was produced domestically, not commercially, and no records were kept. Surviving quilted textiles, however, are made of fabrics manufactured up to about 1890, with only a few quilted pieces using fabrics manufactured later. There were few incentives for spending time on quilting projects. Paris fashions, ready-made and transported by railroad, were desirable, accessible, and inexpensive. Factories turned out warm, inexpensive blankets. Efforts by the poet Frédéric Mistral and others to celebrate Provençal culture helped preserve many customs and traditions but could not withstand the force and bounty of technological change. Isolated groups of women—old women and country folk—were faithful to their *jupons,* but young moderns preferred Gibson girl silhouettes and the fashions that followed. By the time World War I began, the old ways of quilting in Provence were practically nonexistent.

Only recently, with renewed interest in Provence's heritage, have *jupons* for festival days and quilted bedcovers as decorative pieces returned to favor. Eighteenth- and nineteenth-century bedcovers from Provence now hang on the walls of chic Paris apartments and decorate sofas and tables of elegant country homes. Contemporary French quilters take courses in traditional corded, stuffed, and quilted work in Provence and Paris. But the French revival of interest in quilting now encompasses the creative pieced-work quilting traditions of Britain and America. The several thousand members of the Association Française du Patchwork use their needles to recreate the intricate mosaics, appliquéd floral baskets, and geometric pieced-work patterns of other cultures: Ocean Waves, Schoolhouse Blocks, and Log Cabins. Only when they quilt these pieced tops with batting and backing do they return to the roots of their own quilting tradition.

Provençal quilters left a rich and beautiful needlework heritage, unique to their region. All-white, whole-cloth Marseilles corded work is one of the most beautiful and refined arts to emerge from any needlework tradition. The three-dimensional properties of early Marseilles work often referred to as "embroidery from within" inspired a continued exploration of high-relief quilting techniques by domestic needlewomen in Provence. No other quilting tradition in the world can take pride in a similar manipulation of the surface height of cloth with needle, thread, and batting—to glorious sculptural effect. The wealth of corded, stuffed, and quilted works that resulted and were preserved in antique armoires and are now on view in Provençal museums is quite rare and absolutely wonderful.

THE GOLDEN HUES *of a sunflower field in Provence come to life
in this fenêtre (window) quilt. A double-line diamond-grid quilting pattern
with a central star and hearts in all four corners is framed by a flower print border.*

Quilting Projects

THOSE WHO ARE SEDUCED BY THE *beauty of French quilted needlework and who are skilled with a needle can choose among the following ten projects traditional to the Provençal repertoire. They appear in the order of difficulty, from a reversible bedcover to an elaborate whitework wedding quilt.* ❧ *Materials identified in the instructions are ones that will reproduce the original antique piece shown. However, confident quilters may opt to change the fabrics from cotton to silk or vice versa, to enlarge the size of the piece, or even to vary the selection of motifs—all to personalize their work. (Note that silk fabrics, because they are slippery, are more difficult to work with.) Use the Internet to find sources of supplies, such as fine cotton cording and silk batting. If all else fails, supplies can be obtained at Le Rouvray, 3 rue de la Boucherie, 75005, Paris, France, or www.lerouvray.com.* ❧ *Marie-Christine Flocard, an experienced instructor in French quilted needlework, has provided step-by-step information for these ten quilted items.*

A NINETEENTH-CENTURY PROVENÇAL VANNE features a top made of a kashmir cone print, a favorite pattern of the time, and is backed with a contrasting print. Instructions for quilting this small bedcover (see pages 156–59) along with nine other traditional Provençal pieces are provided in this chapter.

Provençal Print Vanne

This project is a simple reversible quilt patterned after a nineteenth-century Provençal *vanne*, a small cover made to rest on top of a bed for decorative effect. It features complementary top and bottom fabrics. The body's inner quilting is a double-line diamond grid, with the border finished in seven rows of parallel stitching lines for a corded-look edge. High-quality complementary fabrics are of the utmost importance to success with a simple quilted piece such as this.

MATERIALS

4 yards (4 m) cotton print fabric for the quilt top

4 yards (4 m) complementary cotton print fabric for the quilt bottom

cotton batting to measure 64 × 72 inches (163 cm × 183 cm)

quilting thread in a color complementary to the prints

100% cotton thread for seams in a matching color

quilting needle

dressmaker pins

straightedge

#2 pencil

quilting frame

FINISHED SIZE: 60 × 68 inches (152 cm × 173 cm) (slightly smaller than a twin sheet). All seams are ¼ inch (6 mm).

1. Trim the selvages from all fabric. Prewash the fabric and iron flat.

2. Cut and seam the top and bottom fabrics into rectangles measuring 62 × 70 inches (157 × 178 cm) (slightly larger than the finished piece). Do not place the seams in the middle of the work, as they will draw too much attention. Match the print pattern at the seams. Press open all seams.

3. To round off the corners, trace a quarter circle in each corner using a compass with a 4-inch (10-cm)

TO MAKE A NICELY ROUNDED CORNER, trace a quarter circle on each corner of the top fabric, using a compass with a 4-inch (10-cm) radius or a plate with an 8-inch (20-cm) diameter, and then trim. Mark and trim the corners of the backing fabric in the same way.

radius or a plate with an 8-inch (20-cm) diameter. Trim to the traced line.

4. Using the straightedge, lightly trace quilting lines on the top fabric. Set the lines on the diagonal, spaced 2½ inches (6 cm) apart, with the second line of quilting set ½ inch (1 cm) lower and to the right of the first line. The seven parallel lines of quilting in the 3½-inch (9-cm) border are also spaced ½ inch (1 cm) apart.

5. Layer together the top, batting, and bottom. Pin and baste, starting from the middle of the quilt and working toward the sides, setting basting lines about every 10 inches (25 cm), up and down and side to side. Baste along the edges.

6. Mount the project in the quilting frame to ensure a consistent tension in the quilting thread. Begin stitching in the center, always working toward the edges. Use a running stitch at 6 to 8 stitches per inch (2 to 3 stitches per cm). Finish the grid quilting in the body of the quilt before starting the border. Make sure that these final stitching lines are parallel and straight. Remove the basting stitches.

7. To finish, trim the top and bottom ½ inch (1 cm) from the outer line of quilting. Trim the batting seam to ¼ inch (6 mm) from the outer line of quilting. Fold the outer edges of both the top and the bottom inside by ¼ inch (6 mm), baste loosely, and then stitch with a small running stitch as close to the edge as possible.

KEEP TOP, BATTING, AND BACKING FABRICS SMOOTH when basting (left) and ease in fullness around corners. THE CORDED-LOOK BORDER (right) is the last step in finishing the vanne. Carefully pin along stitching lines before working with needle and thread.

THE DECORATIVE APPEAL *of this quilted throw begins with the delightful print*
and is enhanced by the quilting motifs, which show a double-line diamond grid in the body
framed by seven rows of parallel line quilting—traditional to almost all Provençal pieces.

159

Reversible Provençal Print Fenêtre

This irresistible charmer is a traditional item in Provençal domestic decor. The quilt features a Provençal floral print framed with a border of silky smooth sateen-weave gold cotton—a composition known as a *fenêtre* (window). The quilting in the body is a simple grid pattern, because a more complicated motif would get lost in the distracting print. The border holds a small assortment of typical Provençal motifs, composed of stylized flowers, puffs, and herbal forms that show well against the cotton sateen. The wonderful surprise of the original piece is the reverse side, another *fenêtre* composition, which is almost shocking in a choice of prints that reflect the more eccentric taste of the turn of the nineteenth century.

MATERIALS

1½ yards (1½ m) cotton print fabric for the quilt top

2¾ yards (2¾ m) plain color sateen-weave cotton for the top border

1½ yards (1½ m) cotton print fabric for the quilt bottom

2¾ yards (2¾ m) cotton print fabric for the bottom border

cotton batting to measure 64 × 72 inches (163 × 183 cm)

quilting thread of a color complementary to the prints

100% cotton thread for seams

quilting needle

dressmaker pins

textile transfer paper

straightedge

#2 pencil

quilting frame

FINISHED SIZE: approximately 60 × 72 inches (152 × 183 cm) (slightly smaller than a twin sheet). All seams are ¼ inch (6 mm).

1. Trim the selvages from all fabric. Prewash the fabric and iron flat.

2. Cut the cotton print for the quilt top to a rectangle measuring 39 × 51 inches (100 × 130 cm). Mark the center of each side with a pin or a light pencil line. Cut the plain sateen-weave cotton into two rectangles for the borders, each measuring 11½ × 61 inches (30 × 155 cm), and two additional rectangles, each measuring 11½ × 73 inches (30 × 185 cm). One border may be pieced, which is common in Provençal quilts. Mark the center of each border piece along one side with a pin or a light pencil line.

3. Cut the cotton print for the quilt bottom to a rectangle measuring 40 × 52 inches (102 × 132 cm), slightly larger than the quilt top. Mark the center of

each side with a pin or a light pencil line. Cut the plain sateen-weave cotton into two rectangles for the borders, each measuring 12 × 61½ inches (31 × 156 cm), and two additional borders, each measuring 12 × 73½ inches (31 × 187 cm). Again, one border may be pieced. Mark the center of each border piece along one side with a pin or a light pencil line.

4. Working with the fabrics for the top, stitch the two shorter borders to the top and bottom of the cotton print, matching the center marks. Press the seams toward the borders. Stitch the two longer borders to the sides of the cotton print and the other borders, matching the center marks. Press all seams toward the borders.

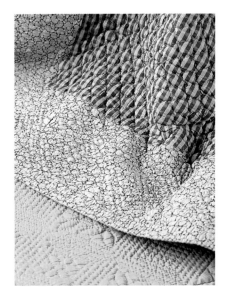

5. Follow the same steps to assemble the bottom fabrics.

6. Using the straightedge, lightly trace the center panel grid quilting lines on the top fabric, according to the quilting pattern shown.

7. On a photocopier, enlarge the illustration 900 percent. (You can begin by doubling the size of the pattern and doubling it again as needed, adjusting the final percentage until the desired enlargement is reached. Even if the resulting image is not totally sharp, it will still be usable.) Following instructions for the transfer paper, copy the enlarged pattern onto the transfer paper and then onto the top sateen-weave border.

8. Layer together the top, batting, and bottom. Pin and baste, starting from the middle of the quilt and working toward the sides, setting basting lines about every 10 inches (25 cm), up and down and side to side. Baste along the edges.

9. Mount the project in the quilting frame to ensure a consistent tension in the quilting thread. Begin stitching in the center, always working toward the edges. Use a running stitch at 6 to 8 stitches per inch (2 to 3 stitches per cm). Finish the grid quilting before starting the floral-motif border. Make sure that these final stitching lines are parallel and straight. Remove the basting stitches.

10. To finish, trim the top and bottom ½ inch (1 cm) from the outer line of quilting. Trim the batting seam to ¼ inch (6 mm) from the outer line of quilting. Fold the outer edges of both the top and the bottom inside by ¼ inch (6 mm), baste loosely, and then stitch with a small running stitch as close to the edge as possible.

Solid-colored Couvre-lit

Similar to the *vanne*, this *couvre-lit* features complementary fabric on each side. However, it is stitched in solid-colored rather than printed cotton to draw full attention to the decorative quilted patterns. The body quilting is a special double-line square grid set on the diagonal, referred to as a *tommettes* pattern because it resembles the tiles often used for paving floors and garden terraces in Provence. The three-tier border is stitched with an inner motif of laurel leaves, a middle pattern of undulating waves, and an outer pattern of open blossoms. This quilt is filled with silk batting; polyester batting may be substituted, but cotton batting should be avoided, because one layer does not provide the necessary loft and two layers result in a heavy bedcover. The original nineteenth-century *couvre-lit* on which this pattern is based has gold cotton on one side and sea green cotton on the other—perhaps reflecting two major life-giving influences on Provençal life: the sun and the sea.

MATERIALS

5 yards (4¾ m) gold cotton fabric for the quilt top

5 yards (4¾ m) sea green cotton fabric for the quilt bottom

silk batting to measure 88 inches (224 cm) square

gold quilting thread

100% cotton thread for seams in a complementary color

quilting needle

dressmaker pins

textile transfer paper

straightedge

#2 pencil

quilting frame

FINISHED SIZE: approximately 87 inches square (221 cm) (same size as a full sheet). All seams are ¼ inch (6 mm).

1. Trim the selvages from all fabric. Prewash the fabric and iron flat.

2. Cut and seam the top and bottom fabrics into 88-inch (224-cm) squares, which will be slightly larger than the finished piece. Do not place seams in the middle of the work, where they would draw too much attention. Press open the seams.

3. On a photocopier, enlarge the border motif shown in the quilting pattern 1300 percent; begin at at any corner and make sure to include two full "waves." Following instructions for the transfer paper, copy the enlarged pattern onto the transfer paper and then onto the top fabric. Begin the transfer at each corner and work sequentially to the right, matching a completed "wave" on the fabric with one on the pattern

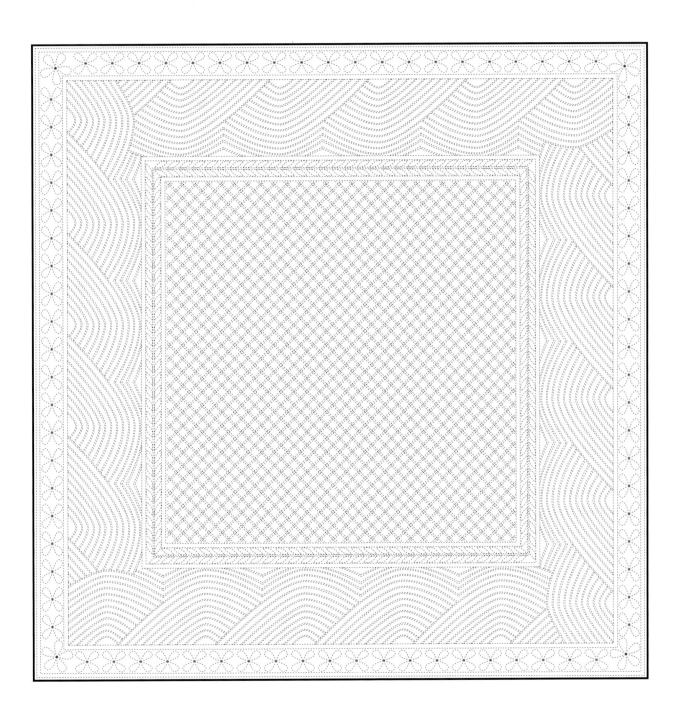

PROVENÇAL GOLD MARRIES THE COLOR OF THE MEDITERRANEAN SEA
in the cottons used for this bedcover (below). Similar typically Provençal quilting
motifs of flowers and bands of laurel leaves are set off by curves that mimic waves.

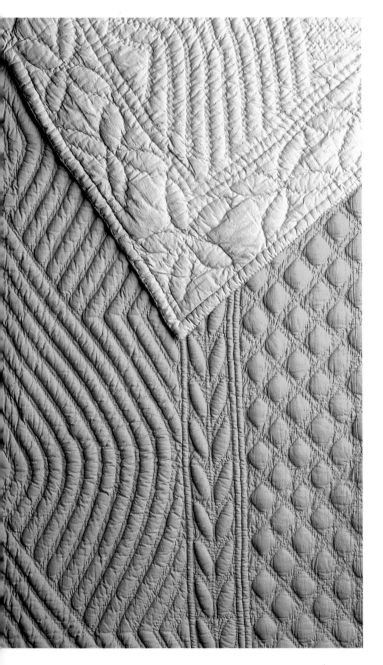

before starting to mark the next "wave." Trace the pattern around the entire border, adjusting as necessary to accommodate the corners.

4. To mark the center *tommettes* pattern, use the straightedge and the pencil to lightly trace the quilting lines in a grid measuring 1½ × 1½ inches (4 × 4 cm). Mark a second set of lines ½ inch (1 cm) lower and to the right of the first set. This will result in the double-line *tommettes* pattern traditional to Provençal quilts.

5. Layer together the top, batting, and bottom. Pin and baste, starting from the middle of the quilt and working toward the sides, setting basting lines about every 10 inches (25 cm), up and down and side to side. Baste along the edges.

6. Mount the project in the quilting frame to ensure a consistent tension in the quilting thread. Begin stitching in the center with a running stitch, always working toward the edges. Finish the grid quilting in the body of the quilt before beginning on the borders. Make sure that these final stitching lines are parallel and straight. Remove basting stitches.

7. To finish, trim the top and the bottom ½ inch (1 cm) from the outer line of quilting. Trim the batting seam to ¼ inch (6 mm) from the outer line of quilting. Fold the outer edges of both the top and the bottom inside by ¼ inch (6 mm), baste loosely, and then stitch with a small running stitch as close to the edge as possible.

PLACED ON A BED SURROUNDED BY WINDOWS, the bedcover (opposite)
is highly decorative. Filled with high-loft silk batting, it is also warm.
Polyester batting will achieve the same warmth and loft.

Silk Couvre-lit Piqué

This is a true confection in pale-colored silk that dates to mid-nineteenth-century Provence. The motifs show an orderly profusion of Provençal fruits and flowers, including fritillaria, tulips, daisies, and melons mingled with exotic stylized herbal forms. The lavender silk is the featured side, while the plain brown cotton backing usefully serves to anchor the quilt on the bed. A silk backing would allow it to slide off, particularly because it is filled with a lightweight silk batting. The silk fabric of this piece is the perfect medium to catch the play of light and shadow and reveal the intricacy of the abundant floral motifs.

MATERIALS

3¾ yards (3½ m) lavender silk for the quilt top

4 yards (3¾ m) brown cotton fabric for the quilt bottom

silk batting to measure 60 × 67 inches (152 × 170 cm)

lavender cotton thread or quilting thread

100% cotton thread in lavender for seams

quilting needle

dressmaker pins

textile transfer paper

#2 pencil

quilting frame

FINISHED SIZE: approximately 57 × 64 inches (145 × 163 cm) (a bed throw). All seams are ¼ inch (6 mm).

1. Trim the selvages from the lavender silk. Cut and seam the silk into a rectangle measuring 60 × 66 inches (152 × 168 cm). Do not place a seam in the middle of the rectangle, where it would draw too much attention. Press open the seams.

2. Trim the selvages from the cotton bottom fabric. Prewash and iron it flat. Cut and seam the cotton into a rectangle measuring 62 × 68 inches (157 × 173 cm), which is slightly larger than the top panel of the quilt. Again, do not place the seam in the middle of the rectangle. Press open the seams.

3. On a photocopier, enlarge the quilting pattern 800 percent. Following instructions for the transfer paper, copy the pattern onto the transfer paper and then onto the silk.

4. Layer together the top, batting, and bottom. Pin and baste, starting from the middle of the quilt and working toward the sides, setting basting lines as wide apart as manageable, up and down and side to side. Needle holes made in the silk during basting will be permanent.

5. Mount the project in the quilting frame to ensure a consistent tension in the quilting thread. Begin stitching in the center, always working toward the edges. Stitch all motifs in a running stitch about 6 to

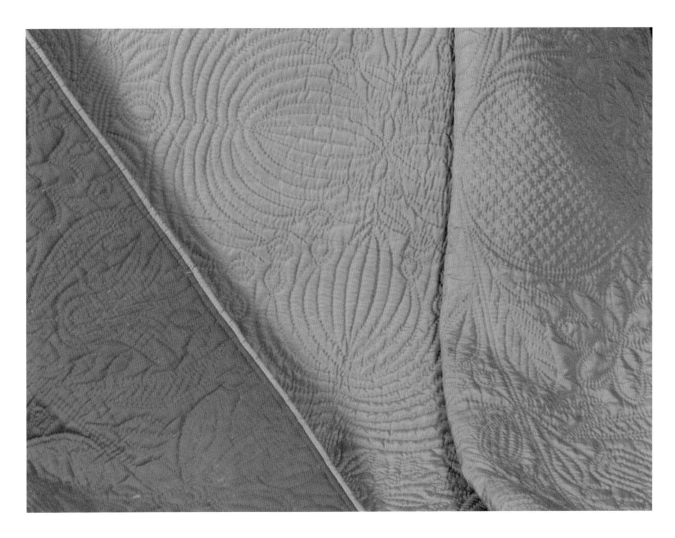

8 stitches per inch (2 to 3 stitches per cm). Make sure that these final stitching lines are parallel and straight. Remove basting stitches.

6. To finish, trim the top and the bottom ½ inch (1 cm) from the outer line of quilting. Trim the batting seam to ¼ inch (6 mm) from the outer line of quilting. Fold the outer edges of both the top and the bottom inside by ¼ inch (6 mm), baste loosely, and then stitch with a small running stitch as close to the edge as possible.

*ALL THE ABUNDANCE of Provence is reflected in this lavender silk bedcover,
carefully rendered in quilted motifs. This piece is perfect for its original use—
placed on the top of a bed for decorative effect, where it can catch ambient light.*

Fenêtre Rouge et Noir

This dramatic beauty, which dates to about 1890 and is made in the typical Provençal *fenêtre* (window) composition, represents the most complicated piecework commonly found in the French needlework tradition. The *fenêtre* was meant to rest on top of a bed for decorative effect. Its backing is a plain-weave red cotton that anchors the slippery silk quilt on the bed, but the entire work is as light as a feather. The focal fabric of this exquisite composition is the scarlet red silk damask, which forms the top of the quilt. Its textured weave adds richness and depth to the surface and draws the eye to the artfully worked vase of flowers. This richness continues in the stunning black silk border quilted with garlands of fruits and flowers.

MATERIALS

1 yard (1 m) scarlet red silk damask for the quilt top

1⅝ yards (1½ m) black plain-weave silk for the top border

3½ yards (3¼ m) red cotton fabric for the quilt bottom

silk batting to measure 54 × 59 inches (140 × 150 cm)

100% cotton red thread

100% cotton black thread

quilting needle

dressmaker pins

textile transfer paper for the red silk

textile carbon paper for the black silk

#2 pencil

quilting frame

FINISHED SIZE: 52 × 57 inches (132 × 145 cm) (a bed throw). All seams are ¼ inch (6 mm).

1. Trim the selvages from the red silk. Cut the silk to a rectangle measuring 30½ × 35½ inches (77.5 × 90 cm). Mark the center of each side with a pin or a light pencil line. Cut the black silk into two borders, each measuring 11½ × 30 inches (30 × 77 cm), and two additional borders, each measuring 11½ × 57½ inches (30 × 146 cm). Mark the center of each border along one side with a pin or a light pencil line.

2. Trim the selvages from the cotton bottom fabric. Prewash and iron it flat. Cut the cotton into two equal lengths; seam the long sides together. Trim this panel to approximately 55 × 61 inches (140 × 155 cm), which is slightly larger than the top panel of the quilt. Do not place a seam in the middle of the rectangle, where it would draw too much attention. Press open the seam. Mark the centers of the top, bottom, and two sides with pins or the pencil.

3. Stitch the two shorter borders to the top and the bottom of the red silk rectangle, matching the center

marks. Press the seams toward the borders. Stitch the two longer borders to the sides of the red silk and the black border, matching the center marks. Press all seams toward the border.

4. On a photocopier, enlarge the quilting pattern 750 percent. Following instructions for the transfer paper, copy the pattern onto the transfer paper and then onto the silk.

5. Layer together the top, bottom, and batting. Pin and baste, starting from the middle of the quilt and working toward the sides, setting basting lines as wide apart as manageable, up and down and side to side. Needle holes made in the silk during basting will be permanent.

6. Mount the project in the quilting frame to ensure a consistent tension in the quilting thread. Begin stitching in the center, always working toward the edges. Use red thread on the red fabric and black thread on the black fabric. Stitch all motifs in a running stitch. Make sure that these final stitching lines are parallel and straight. Remove basting stitches.

7. To finish, trim the top and the bottom ¼ inch (6 mm) from the outer line of quilting. Trim the batting seam to ½ inch (1 cm) from the outer line of quilting. Fold the outer edges of both the top and the bottom inside by ¼ inch (6 mm), baste loosely, and then stitch with a small running stitch as close to the edge as possible.

RED AND BLACK create an unusual combination of colors for a Provençal quilt, but the effect is striking. The present owner has mounted it like artwork on his dining room wall.

Broderie de Marseille Technique

Quilters are advised to try a small practice piece when they attempt to work in the *broderie de Marseille* (corded and stuffed needlework) technique used for the five quilting projects that follow.

MATERIALS

100% cotton or silk fabric (best quality), depending on the project

thin white cotton needle-punch batting, such as Mountain Mist White Rose

white cotton cording ⅟16 or ³⁄16 inch (2 or 5 mm) in diameter (substitution: good-quality, firmly twisted white cotton knitting yarn)

100% cotton thread, such as DMC #40, or quilting thread

narrow white cotton bias tape, if the project has curved edges

tapestry needle #20 or #22

trapunto needle

quilting needle #10

quilting or embroidery hoop

toothpicks

tracing paper

black fine-point felt-tip pen

#2 pencil

Cutting (STEP A)

1. Cut two identical pieces of fabric, one for the top and one for the bottom. Do not prewash them.

Construction (STEP B)

1. On a photocopier, enlarge the project pattern to the dimension indicated in the project instructions.

2. Transfer the enlarged pattern to the tracing paper with the felt-tip pen.

3. Iron the fabric perfectly flat.

4. To center the pattern, lightly trace four lines with the pencil on the right side of the fabric. Draw two diagonal lines from each corner to its opposite and two lines across the middle, forming an "×" from top to bottom and a "+" from side to side.

5. Pin the tracing-paper pattern under the fabric, matching the centers. Lightly trace the entire design with the pencil.

Assembly (STEP C)

1. Place the top piece on the bottom piece with wrong sides together. Pin and baste, starting from the middle and working toward the sides. Set basting lines about every 10 inches (25 cm), up and down and side to side. Baste along the edges.

THE SMALL SCALE OF PATTERN MOTIFS in an early-eighteenth-century broderie de Marseille bedcover is illustrated by the juxtaposition of a thimble. The patterns are worked in a simple running stitch, at approximately twenty-four stitches per inch, that caught only two or three threads of the top fabric at a time.

2. Loosely insert the project into the hoop, right side up. Allow some ease; if the fabric is too taught it will be difficult to insert the cording.

3. Starting from the center and working toward the borders, stitch along all compartment and channel pattern lines of the central design, using a small running stitch or a back-stitch as the project requires. The stitches should be as small as possible, on the order of 10 to 12 per inch (4 to 5 per cm) Stitch through both layers of fabric; hide the knots inside the two layers. Complete the central design before working on outer borders.

Stuffing (STEP D)

1. Remove the project from the hoop and work on a flat surface.

2. Beginning at the center, use the tip of a needle to separate the threads of the bottom fabric to make a small hole under a pattern compartment. Try not to break the bottom threads, and do not cut the fabric.

3. Cut the needle-punch batting into strips 5 inches (15 cm) long and 3/16 inch (5 mm) wide. Gently push a batting strip into the design compartment with a toothpick. Close the hole by scratching the threads back into place with a sharp pin. Continue until all compartments are plump and firm. This process will require extraordinary patience and skill. Stuff all compartments before inserting the cording. Be assured that the tiny holes made by the needle will disappear in the final washing.

Cording (STEP E)

1. Begin at the center of the work, wrong side up. Separate the threads of the bottom fabric with the tip of the needle at the beginning and the end of the first channel to be filled. Try not to break the bottom threads, and do not cut the fabric.

2. Thread a tapestry needle #20 with a length of cotton

cording 2 inches (5 cm) longer than the channel to be filled. To thread the needle with the *lasso* technique, cut a 15-inch (38-cm) length of quilting thread, double it, and insert it into the eye of the needle. Catch the length of cording in the loop made by the doubled thread, and ease the cording gently through the needle eye.

3. Work the needle through the channel and gently ease the cording into position. Use a tapestry needle for short channels and a trapunto needle for longer channels. Based on the width of the channels, one or two strands of cording will be required. Draw the cording through the channel, making sure to leave an inch (2.5 cm) of cording at the entrance of the channel and clipping the cording an inch (2.5 cm) longer than the end of the channel.

4. Gently adjust the tension of the cording inside the channel until it lays flat. Clip the cording at each end of the channel, leaving a small tail. Poke the cording tails into the ends of the channels with a toothpick. Close the hole by scratching the threads back together. Continue to fill the channels one by one.

5. To fill a channel with a reverse curve, work a hole in the middle of the curve, draw the needle out, and settle the cording into the channel. Reenter the channel through the same hole to fill the remaining part of the curve. Gently draw the cording through, mindful not to distort the first half of the curve.

Edges (STEP F)

There are two methods for finishing the edges of a piece worked in *broderie de Marseille*.

a. Trim the edges of the bottom to 3/16 inch (5 mm) from the last line of stitching. Trim the edges of the front to within 1/2 inch (1 cm) of the last line of stitching. Fold in these seam allowances, carefully clipping the curves. Blind stitch along the outer edge, working wrong side up; or

b. Trim the edges of both the top and the bottom to 1/4 inch (6 mm) from the last line of stitching. Fold the seam allowance to the wrong side. Blind stitch a narrow white bias tape along the outer edge. Finish by blind stitching the other edge of the bias tape to the bottom, making sure that the seam allowance is covered.

Finishing (STEP G)

To finish projects made of cotton, wash the piece in tepid water with a neutral, pH-balance soap. Rinse fastidiously. Roll in a white towel to absorb excess water. Lay flat to dry, smoothing the piece every once in awhile. Do not iron. This final step will eliminate the holes made by the needle, remove the pencil marks, and nestle the cording into the design compartments and channels.

Corded Bib

This charming infant bib made with the *broderie de Marseille* technique was probably used for social occasions. It features motifs of pearls and blooming rosemary—signifying wealth and familial love for the baby. The original piece was made using only cording, even to fill the compartments that create the floral and pearl motifs. Although purists may want to try this, others may find it easier to use needle-punch batting when filling these small compartments.

MATERIALS

½ yard (46 cm) fine-quality white cotton fabric

⅛ yard (12 cm) thin white cotton needle-punch batting cut into strips ³⁄₁₆ × 5 inches (5 mm × 15 cm)

15 yards (15 m) white cotton cording ³⁄₁₆ inch (5 mm) in diameter

100% cotton white thread, such as DMC #40 or quilting thread

1 yard (1 m) narrow cotton bias tape

1 small white button

tapestry needle #20 or #22

trapunto needle

quilting needle #10

quilting or embroidery hoop

toothpicks

tracing paper

black fine-point felt-tip pen

#2 pencil

FINISHED SIZE: approximately 7 × 9 inches (18 × 23 cm)

1. Cut the fabric into two rectangles large enough to fit into the hoop (at least 9 × 11 inches) (23 × 28 cm).

2. Follow step B in the *broderie de Marseille* instructions. On a photocopier, enlarge the illustration 115 percent.

3. At step C, fill the compartments for the flower, rosemary leaves, and pearls before going on to the other design motifs; use either cording (as in the original) or needle-punch batting strips for ease.

4. Continue with steps D through F; use the second method to trim and finish the edges.

5. Wash according to instructions in step G.

6. Sew the button on one side of the back. Make a loop using the buttonhole stitch on the other side of the back.

THIS TINY BIB *is not as impractical as it may appear.*
When an infant is presented to society, the bib can catch baby spills
that might otherwise stain a gown. It is easier to wash a bib than fine linen.

Petassoun with Diamond and Grape Motif

This small traditional quilt was made to protect a new mother's dress from her infant during special occasions, such as a christening or when friends came to call. In this item, which dates from about 1850, a central diamond puff motif is enclosed in a curved and scalloped frame that ends in three puffs on each point. An eight-point garland of rosemary sprays surrounds the inner diamond. Four points of the garland end in grape bunches, while four meet the scalloped outer border. All motifs lie on a field of diagonal corded lines. The scalloped edge holds inner scallops formed by twists of cording.

MATERIALS

1 yard (1 m) fine-quality white cotton fabric

⅛ yard (12 cm) thin white cotton needle-punch batting cut into strips ³⁄₁₆ × 5 inches (5 mm × 15 cm)

15 yards (15 m) white cotton cording ¹⁄₁₆ or ³⁄₁₆ inch (2 or 5 mm) in diameter

100% cotton white thread, such as DMC #40, or quilting thread

3 yards (3 m) narrow cotton bias tape

tapestry needle #20 or #22

trapunto needle

quilting needle #10

quilting or embroidery hoop

toothpicks

tracing paper

black fine-point felt-tip pen

#2 pencil

FINISHED SIZE: approximately 19 × 18 inches (49 × 46 cm)

1. Cut the fabric into two squares large enough to fit into the hoop (at least 22 inches square) (56 cm × 56 cm).

2. Follow steps B and C in the *broderie de Marseille* instructions. The quilting pattern should be enlarged 265 percent.

3. At step D, before working on the diagonal line ground, fill the compartments for the central diamond motif, rosemary leaves, grapes, and pearls using either cording or needle-punch batting strips for ease.

4. Continue with steps E and F, but do not fill the compartments for the puffed border until the end; use the second method to trim and finish the edges.

5. Wash according to instructions in step G.

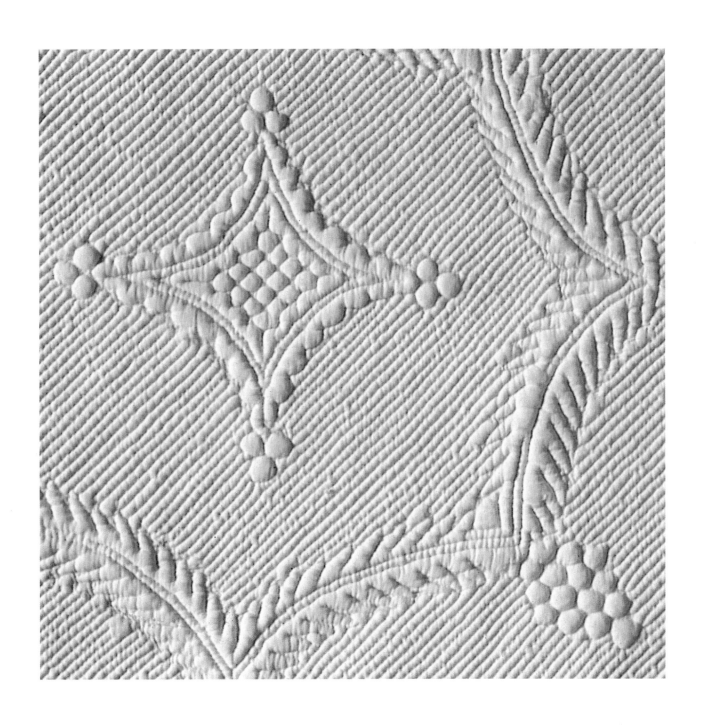

*THIS PETASSOUN REPRESENTS the corded broderie de Marseille tradition,
which flourished in Marseilles three hundred years ago and was continued by skilled
needlewomen in fishing villages along the Mediterranean coast until World War I.*

Broderie de Marseille Pillow Sham

This *oreiller* (pillow sham) from about 1775 shows an elaborate monogram under a crown, all set in a frame of floral forms; a ribbon-tied bouquet of flowers occupies each corner. It is worked in back stitch in the *broderie de Marseille* technique. Although this piece was found as an unfinished fragment, pillow shams like this were often trimmed with lace or fringe. Queen Marie Lescynska, the wife of Louis XV, had eighteen pillow shams worked in *broderie de Marseille* for her summer furnishings at Fontainebleau, according to notes made in 1750 by the duke de Luynes; hers were trimmed with lace.

MATERIALS

1¼ yards (1¼ m) fine-quality white cotton fabric

100% cotton white thread, such as DMC #40 or quilting thread

150 yards (140 m) white cotton cording ⅟16 inch (2 mm) in diameter

optional trim: 2½ yards (2½ m) lace or fringe

optional sham closures: hook with loop tape, buttons, or snaps

tapestry needle #20 or #22

trapunto needle

quilting needle #10

quilting or embroidery hoop

toothpicks

tracing paper

black fine-point felt-tip pen

#2 pencil

FINISHED SIZE: approximately 17 × 22 inches (44 × 56 cm).

1. Trim the selvages from the cotton fabric. Cut the cotton into two rectangles, each 19 × 24 inches (49 × 61 cm). (The two top pieces of fabric are larger than the finished project to allow for the shrinking that accompanies the corded technique.) Save the remaining white cotton for use as the sham backing.

2. On a photocopier, enlarge the pillow sham pattern 250 percent. Transfer the enlarged pattern to the tracing paper with the felt-tip pen.

3. Iron perfectly flat the two rectangles for the top. To center the pattern, lightly trace four lines with the pencil on the right side of the fabric. Draw two diagonal lines from each corner to its opposite and two lines across the middle, forming an "×" from top to bottom and a "+" from side to side.

4. Pin the tracing-paper pattern under the fabric with the marked lines, matching centers. Lightly trace the entire design on the top fabric.

5. Follow step C in the *broderie de Marseille* instructions.

6. Omit step D, as no batting is used in this piece.

7. Follow step E. The original piece is worked with a back stitch at 10 to 12 stitches per inch (4 to 5 per cm); a running stitch may be substituted. The narrow width of the channel may require use of the *lasso* technique described in step E. An extra row of cording around the edge makes a nice finish.

8. Wash according to instructions in step G. Trim the finished top, allowing a ½-inch (1-cm) seam allowance outside the outer line of stitching. Measure the top. Depending on the stitch tension and the amount of fabric taken up by the cording, it may vary from the finished dimension indicated.

9. Prewash, dry, and iron flat the fabric saved for the bottom. Finish the edge of the short side of each bottom piece by turning under a ½-inch (1 cm) seam allowance. Fold the seam allowance over another 2 inches (5 cm) and blind stitch it in place. Lay one piece wrong side up, then lay the bottom piece on top, finished edges overlapping. Pin at the top and the bottom of the overlap. Turn the bottom right side up. Pin the finished top on the bottom, right sides together. Stitch along all edges. Turn right side out.

10. Add optional closures and trim as desired.

THE FRENCH ARISTOCRACY *filled their bedrooms and dressing areas with luxury textiles worked in broderie de Marseille. In the eighteenth century, they often received guests while in the midst of their toilette.*

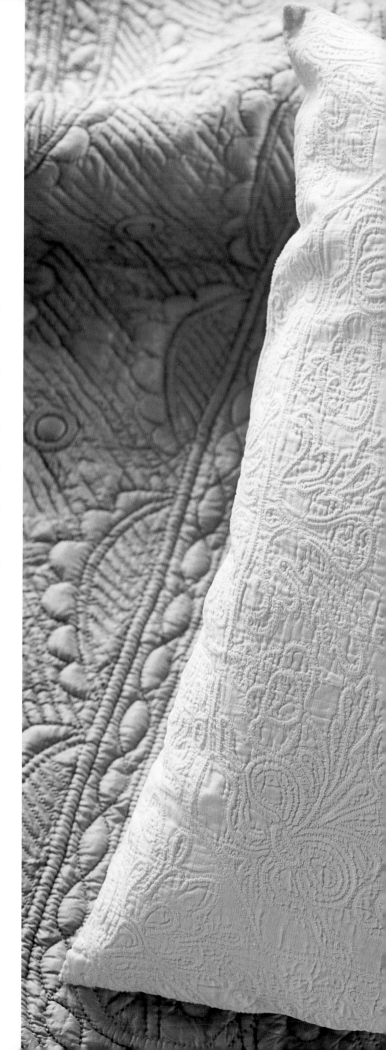

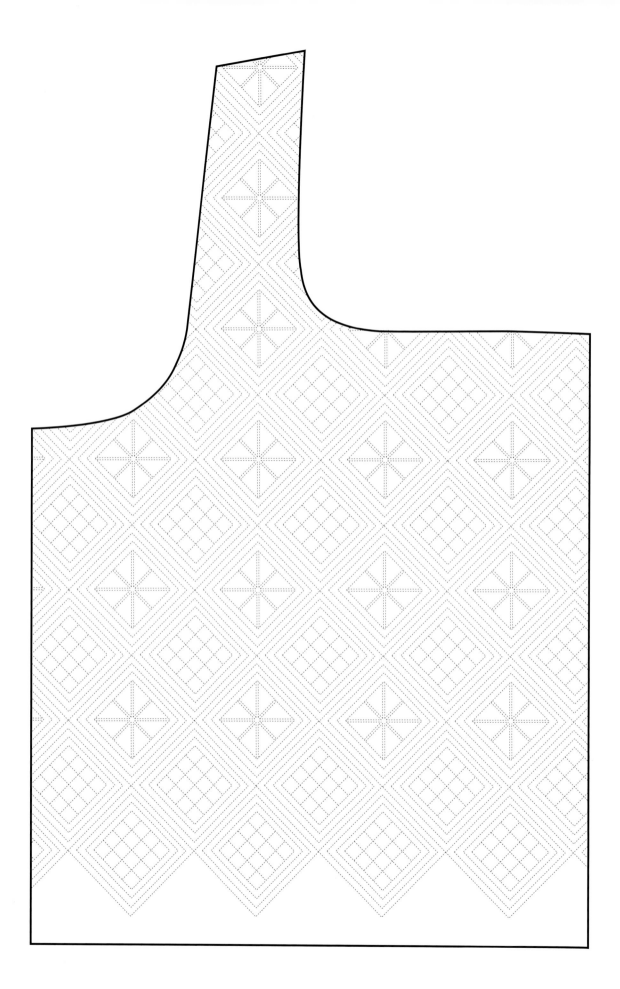

Provençal Corset

This vest represents an integral part of Provençal women's dress from the eighteenth century to World War I (see the women depicted in paintings on pages 1, 6, and 84–85). Fashioned of a pale blue silk worked in the *broderie de Marseille* technique, the costume piece has a lining of coarsely woven linen. The project pattern shows only the organization of motifs. Quilters should find a vest pattern of appropriate size from which to cut the garment pattern. To follow the original style, you may choose to ignore the closure details of the selected pattern and extend the bodice fronts so that they overlap. Traditional closures were simple pins; modern women may prefer snaps.

MATERIALS

1½ yards (1½ m) silk for the outer vest

1½ yards (1½ m) ecru open-weave linen for the lining

30 yards (30 m) white cotton cording ³⁄₁₆ inch (5 mm) in diameter

optional: ⅛ yard (12 cm) thin white cotton needle-punch batting cut into strips ³⁄₁₆ × 5 inches (5 mm × 15 cm)

100% cotton thread to match the silk

tapestry needle #20 or #22

trapunto needle

quilting needle #10

quilting or embroidery hoop

toothpicks

tracing paper

black fine-point felt-tip pen

#2 pencil

PROVENÇAL WOMEN *wore cotton corsets souples (supple bodices)*
for daily use and corsets made of silk for fancier occasions. However, a corset souple,
because of its construction, was more comfortable than boned versions.

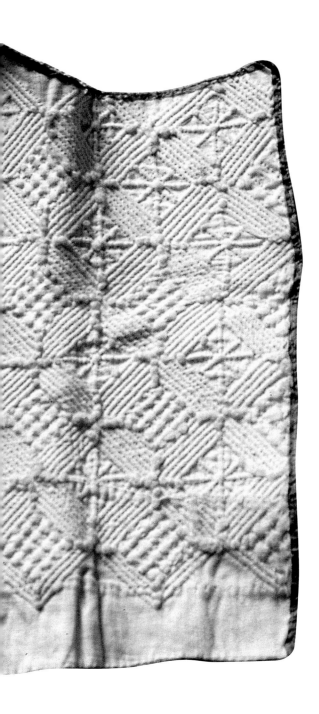

1. Cut the silk into three rectangles. Cut two rectangles large enough to fit the two bodice fronts of the garment pattern, including an extension for the overlap, plus excess to fit in the quilting hoop. Cut the third rectangle large enough to fit the bodice back of the garment pattern, plus excess to fit in the quilting hoop.

2. Cut three pieces of the linen in the same sizes as the silk fabric.

3. Follow step B in the *broderie de Marseille* instructions. Enlarge the illustrated pattern to fit the widest point of the garment pattern bodice. The illustrated pattern will result in an overlap, the width of which depends on individual bust size. Take care to make the tracing lines as minimal as possible, as this garment will not be washed to finish.

4. Follow the instructions for step C, working separately on each bodice section.

5. Follow step D to fill the compartments for the diamond puffs, using either cording or needle-punch batting strips.

6. Follow step E to fill the channels with cording.

7. With the right sides of the silk together, seam the bodice shoulders and sides. Open the bodice and blind stitch the shoulder and side seams of the linen.

8. Finish the neckline, arm holes, and bottom edges with the first method in step F.

9. Add closures.

Vase of Flowers Wedding Quilt

This lovely ceremonial quilt was made to grace the nuptial bed on one's wedding night and dates to the mid-nineteenth century. A central medallion is formed by a laurel wreath framing an ornate vase that holds a magnificent bouquet. The identifiable flowers speak a language of sentiment: roses for true, passionate love, daisies for femininity, and lilies for purity. The medallion rests on a grid of puffed diamonds and flowers, bordered in turn with olives and olive branches, then a swag of rosemary, a daisy border, and finally six rows of parallel cording.

Laurel, olives, and rosemary are significant in Provençal tradition. When the poet Petrarch lived in the Vaucluse, he planted a laurel tree to honor his beloved *Laure* and wrote sonnets to her under its branches. In several valleys of the Basse-Alpes, a young woman would cut a leaf of laurel and incise on it the names of several marriageable young men. She kept the leaf tucked over her heart until evening, when she examined the leaf to see which name had darkened the most—for that would be the name of her future husband. The quilt's olive motifs, which portend richness and abundance, may indicate the bridegroom's occupation. Rosemary is of particular significance given the Provençal saying, "*Au roumanis l'amour es au nis*" ("With rosemary, love is born"). In the village of Cabasse, youths would prepare for the feast day of St. John by decking the village streets with rosemary and broom to perfume the air as they leaped over St. John's Fire and learned whether or not they would marry that year. On the first of May in several villages, a young man would get up at dawn to place a sprig of rosemary on the window sill of his intended. If she accepted his affection, she would plant the sprig in fertile soil and place the pot on the sill.

Made in the *broderie de Marseille* technique, this wedding quilt is recommended for experienced, patient needleworkers. The motifs in the original piece, even the small compartments, are filled with cording. Although purists may want to try this, others may find it easier to use needle-punch batting when forming the tiny puffs.

MATERIALS

3 yards (3 m) fine-quality white cotton fabric, at least 50 inches wide (127 cm)

1 yard (1 m) thin white cotton needle-punch batting cut into strips 3/16 × 5 inches (5 mm × 15 cm)

350 yards (320 m) white cotton cording 1/16 to 3/16 inch (2 to 5 mm) in diameter

100% cotton white thread or quilting thread

tapestry needle #20 or #22

trapunto needle

quilting needle #10

quilting or embroidery hoop

toothpicks

tracing paper

black fine-point felt-tip pen

#2 pencil

A SUMPTUOUS PIECE such as this whitework marriage quilt (below) would be placed on the marital bed the night of a couple's nuptials. After that, it was stored in an armoire for safekeeping until another family wedding.

FINISHED SIZE: 46 × 49 inches (117 × 125 cm) (a bed throw or a wall hanging).

1. Trim the selvages from the white cotton fabric. Cut the fabric into two rectangles, each approximately 50 × 54 inches (127 × 140 cm).

2. Follow steps B and C in the *broderie de Marseille* instructions. On a photocopier, enlarge the pattern illustration 675 percent.

3. At step D, fill the compartments for the flower, the rosemary leaves, and the pearls before going on to other design motifs, using either cording or needle-punch batting strips.

4. Continue with step E.

5. At step F, follow the first method for trimming and finishing the edges.

6. Finish with step G, and congratulate yourself!

THE CENTRAL MEDALLION of this quilt (opposite) shows a profusion of flowers in an elegant footed vase. This voluptuous image portends a fertile and abundant future for the newlyweds. (For a full view of this quilt, see page 120; other views are on pages 61 and 121.)

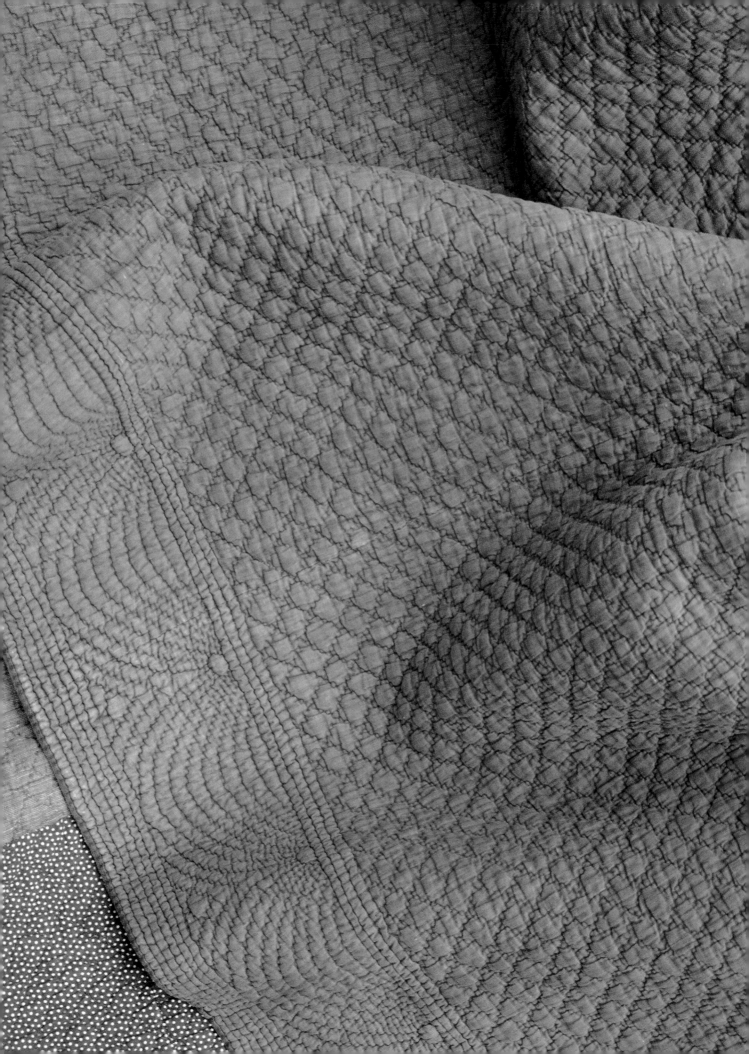

How to Care for and Display Quilts

Antique cotton and silk quilts should be handled with care so that they can be enjoyed by future generations. Their worst enemies are abrasion, strong light, and high heat and humidity. With attention to methods of storage and display they can last for many more years.

How to Care for Quilts

Antique fabrics are often fragile, especially when they hold colored dyes. The basic rules are simple: Keep old textiles away from sunlight and excessive heat. If an old quilt is on a bed next to a window, close the curtains to prevent direct light from striking it every day.

Storing Quilts

Store textiles, quilts, and other linens in cloth bags (old white cotton pillow cases are perfect), not in plastic bags. Old white sheets, prewashed lengths of muslin, and acid-free tissue can also be used. Precious textiles should be stored so that no dyed area touches any other part. When folding them, line the folds with rolls of muslin or tissue. Refold textiles occasionally along different fold lines.

Acid-free boxes are useful for long-term storage. Do not use moth balls to store cottons. Do not store textiles in an attic that overheats in the summer.

Cleaning Quilts

Freshen a quilt by airing it outdoors. Open it flat, face down, on a shady area of grass.

Silk, woolen, and cotton quilts benefit from a gentle cleaning with a vacuum cleaner to remove surface dust and grit. Cover the vacuum head with a piece of screening made from fiberglass, available at any hardware store.

Be reluctant to clean old textiles. Commercial dry cleaning agents damage cotton fibers. Even a gentle water bath causes cotton fibers to expand and contract and should be given sparingly and gently. It is best to seek an expert opinion about cleaning individual quilts.

If you must wash a cotton quilt, follow these guidelines:

1. Test colorfastness by pressing a damp white cloth against all colored textiles. If colors lift onto the white cloth, the dyes are not fast and washing may result in disaster; in this case, consult an expert.

2. Fill the bathtub with tepid water and place the quilt in the tub. Let it soak for about an hour, occasionally pumping gently. If acid has built up in the cottons, it will cause the water to turn yellow-brown as it drains from the fibers. This is not harmful to the quilt. Change the water once or twice until it runs clear. Each time the tub drains, gently push the quilt to the side, away from the drain.

3. After the water runs clear, fill the tub again and for an average-size bed quilt add about ¼ cup of dye-free, perfume-free liquid detergent that has been dissolved in a cup of water. For quilts dating before 1850 use a soap made specially for cleaning old textiles, such as Orvis; do not clean cotton textiles with a product made for silk or woolen textiles. Rinse four or five times to remove all sticky soap residue.

4. Cradle the quilt in an old white sheet and lift it out of the tub, squeezing gently and firmly to remove excess water; take time to remove as much water as possible.

5. To dry, lay the quilt flat on a layer of toweling, either indoors or outdoors but away from direct sunlight. Block it into its previous shape. If indoors, position a small fan over the quilt or place a portable dehumidifier in the room to help the evaporation process. In eight to ten hours the quilt may be

A QUILTED BEDCOVER IN PROVENÇAL BLUE began life at the end of the eighteenth century as a jupon. The drapery swags quilted in the border, which originally circled the hem of the skirt, now decorate each end of the quilt.

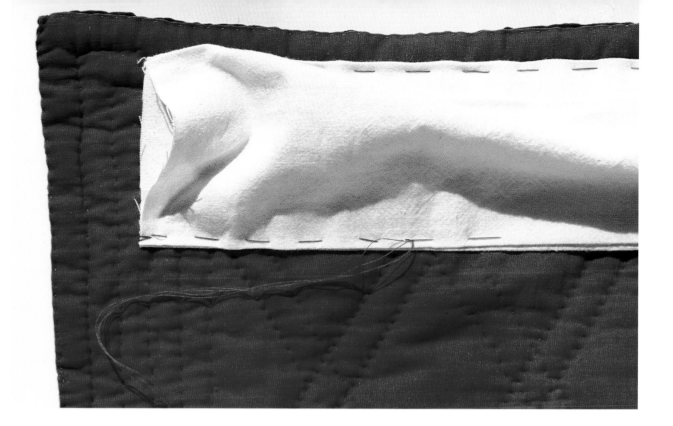

light enough to hang over a rail if absolutely necessary because of space limitations; however, it is better to leave it flat until it dries completely.

Conservation soap, acid-free tissue, and acid-free boxes are available from some museum stores and from Talas, 568 Broadway, New York, N.Y. 10012-9989.

How to Display Quilts

Displaying handsome pieces of quilted needlework is part of the pleasure of owning them. Quilts too precious to be used on a bed can be put on a table or piano top or mounted and displayed on a wall, although always away from direct sunlight.

Using a Sleeve

The simplest and least expensive yet safe way to prepare a quilt for use as a wall hanging is to attach a sleeve.

1. Cut prewashed muslin or sheeting 8 inches wide by the length of the top of the quilt less 2 inches.

2. By hand or machine sew a seam down the length to make a roll or sleeve.

3. Pin the sleeve across the top of the quilt back, ½ inch from the top edge and recessed 1 inch from each side.

4. Using large basting stitches and thread that blends in with the surface textile, stitch the top of the flattened sleeve to the quilt, going through all layers. The stitches may be 1 inch apart on the back and ¼ inch apart on the front.

5. Raise the sleeve and push it up slightly so that when reflattened the top of the sleeve folds over itself and meets the top edge of the quilt. Carefully pin the bottom of the sleeve to the quilt, catching the backing fabric and the batting but not the surface fabric.

6. Make a second line of large basting stitches along the bottom of the sleeve and remove the pins. The front of the sleeve should lie flat against the quilt; the back of the sleeve should

*TO ALLOW THE QUILT TO HANG SMOOTHLY FROM THE MOUNTING, there should be more ease
in the back of the sleeve than in the front. Stitch the top of the sleeve onto the quilt, raise the sleeve
to meet the top of the quilt, and stitch where the bottom of the sleeve falls.*

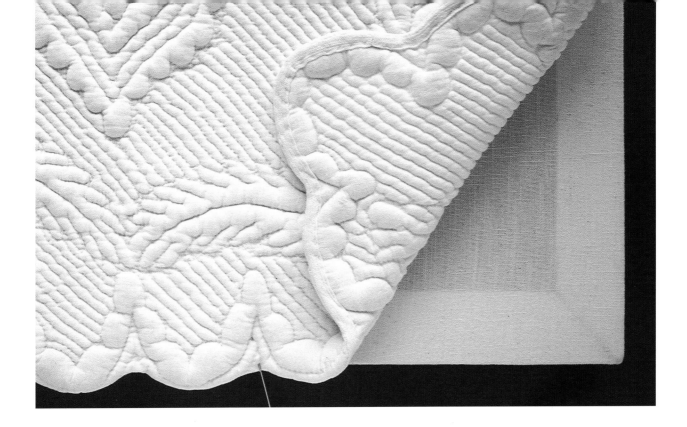

round out away from the quilt to allow a rod or board to be inserted without making a bump on the front.

7. Through the sleeve opening insert a rod or small wooden board 1 inch shorter than the width of the quilt. It will extend beyond the sleeve on each side but will not be noticeable from the front when mounted.

8. Mount the rod on the wall.

9. If the quilt is symmetrical, sew another sleeve on the inside bottom so that the quilt can be rotated twice a year.

Using a Stretcher

Quilts can also be mounted on a wooden stretcher that has been covered with prewashed heavy muslin or canvas.

1. Measure the quilt carefully and make (or have made) a wooden stretcher or frame that allows the quilt to extend about ½ inch on each side. This extension hides the stretcher from view and lessens strain on the outer edge of the quilt.

2. Cover the stretcher with muslin or canvas that has been washed and rinsed several times to make sure that all chemical agents have been removed.

3. Carefully baste the quilt around all sides, going through all layers; use stitches about 1 inch apart on the back side and ¼ inch apart on the surface. If the quilt is large or heavy, tack it every 6 inches or so through the back of the stretcher fabric.

4. Put two hanging wires on the back of the stretcher to allow the quilt to be rotated twice a year.

Using Velcro

Strips of Velcro can be sewn to all sides of a quilt, with the matching strips glued or tacked onto a stretcher or even directly on the wall. Velcro can be stiff and unforgiving but useful if the quilt is shaped more like a trapezoid than a rectangle.

To remove dust and grit from mounted quilts, vacuum through a piece of fiberglass screening twice a year.

BEFORE MOUNTING THE QUILT ON A WOODEN STRETCHER, cover the wooden frame with muslin that has been washed several times. This will protect the textile from damage from the wood and provide a backing to which a quilt can be basted.

Where to See and Buy French Quilts

Examples of exquisite Provençal needlework are dispersed throughout Provence and France. To seek them out for the pure pleasure of seeing them or to purchase them requires some travel and a handy phrase book.

Where to See French Quilts

This section identifies museums, chateaus, and other sites with collections of quilted needlework in Provence, Paris, and other parts of France. For up-to-date information, use an Internet search engine to look for a Web site. Most important, before setting off for one of these destinations, call to make sure that it is open and not closed for renovation. When calling from outside France, dial 33 for the country code, drop the 0, and then dial the last nine digits.

In Provence

Museon Arlaten
29, rue de la République
Arles
04 90 93 58 11
Closed Mondays

When the nineteenth-century poet Frédéric Mistral won the Nobel Prize for literature in 1904, he used his prize money to establish this museum, a celebration of eighteenth- and nineteenth-century life in Provence. Collections include pre-Revolution Provençal costumes and other exquisite examples of the fine work done by professional quilters.

Musée de Vignasse
Château de Beaucaire
Beaucaire
04 66 59 47 61
Closed Tuesdays

A small collection of quilted *jupons* and other textiles is one of this museum's displays of regional folk items. A stop here can be combined with a visit to Tarascon, just across the Rhône River.

Musée des Arts et Traditions Populaires de Draguignan
15, rue Joseph Roumanille
Draguignan (above the Côte d'Azur)
04 94 47 05 72
Closed Mondays

The museum has a lovely exhibit of Provençal quilted costumes, including a bride's ensemble. Quilted textiles are integrated into other aspects of Provençal life to illuminating effect.

Château Grignan
Village center
Grignan (east of Orange)
04 75 91 83 55
Open daily

Textile lovers may want to join literary pilgrims who venture to the Château Grignan, home of the daughter of the renowned seventeenth-century letter-writer Madame Marie de Rabutin Chantal de Sevigné. Madame Marguerite de Grignan received hundreds of letters and several visits from her literate mother at Château Grignan. (In one letter before a visit Madame de Sevigné pleads, "Do try to banish those beastly bed bugs from my room; the very thought of them frightens me to death" (*Madame de Sevigné: Selected Letters*). The chateau holds two sets of magnificent seventeenth-century quilted bed hangings, one in gold silk, the other in a woodblock-printed textile.

Musée des Costumes et de Bijoux Provençales
2, rue Jean Ossola
Grasse
04 93 40 12 04

The delicate allure of eighteenth- and nineteenth-century Provençal costume is manifest in this exquisite collection of feminine attire, from bonnet to slipper.

Musée Charles Deméry
Souleiado Company
39, rue Proudhon
Tarascon
04 90 91 08 80
Open Wednesdays through Sundays

The tour (in English on request) and exhibits present the history of this family-owned textile printing operation. A visit here can be combined with one to Beaucaire, just across the Rhône River.

Musée de Vieux Nîmes
Place aux Herbes
Nîmes
04 66 76 73 70
Closed Mondays and holidays

This museum specializes in decorative arts of the seventeenth and eighteenth centuries. The library has sample books of eighteenth-century cloth printed in Nîmes.

Musée des Civilisations d'Europe
et de la Méditerranée
Marseilles
Open in 2008

This new museum includes the collection from the former Musée des Arts et Traditions Populaires in Paris and often features textiles in special exhibits.

Musée des Arts et Traditions Populaires de Château Gombert
5, Place des Héros
Marseilles
04 91 68 14 38
Closed Tuesdays; call in advance to confirm hours

The museum holds an extraordinary collection of Provençal costume pieces, ranging from a late-seventeenth-century quilted *cotillon* made from an imported *indienne* and an eighteenth-century corded-work camisole of delicate beauty to nineteenth-century *jupons* and *couvre-lits*. Non-textile-oriented companions will be captivated by other museum displays of Provençal life.

Musée des Vallées Cévenoles
95, Grand Rue
St.-Jean-du-Gard (in the Cévennes, near Alès)
04 66 85 10 48
www.museedescevennes.com
Open daily April through October and Tuesdays, Thursdays, and Sundays November to March

Old ways of local silk production are exhibited in detail in the small museum.

Outside Provence

Musée des Tissus
34, rue de la Charité
Lyons
04 78 38 42 00
www.musee-des-tissus.com
Closed Mondays and holidays

This museum presents a fascinating exploration of the history of the silk industry in Lyons, well supported by luscious silk textile exhibits and a few early quilted costume pieces.

Musée de l'Impression sur Étoffes
14, rue Jean-Jacques Henner
Mulhouse
03 89 46 83 00
www.musee-impression.com
Closed Mondays and holidays

This museum, funded by France's textile manufacturers, holds swatch books of thousands of printed textiles produced in this famous textile center as well as around the world. Special exhibits, always strikingly mounted, focus on various aspects of textile printing.

In Paris

Musée des Arts Décoratifs
Palais du Louvre
107, rue de Rivoli
01 44 55 57 50
www.paris.org (click on Musées, then click on the name of the museum)
Closed Mondays and Tuesdays

The Musée des Arts Décoratifs contains a rich collection of French decorative arts. The library holds the Aix-la-Chapelle pattern book, seventy-one swatches of early fabrics assembled in 1807.

Musée des Arts de la Mode et du Textile
Palais du Louvre
107, rue de Rivoli
01 44 55 57 50
www.paris.org (click on Musées, then click on the name of the museum)
Closed Tuesdays

The Musée des Arts de la Mode et du Textile holds rotating costume exhibits, always delightful, but confirm that the museum is open before you go.

Musée de la Mode et du Costume
Palais Galliera
10, avenue Pierre-Ier-de Serbie
01 56 52 86 20
www.galliera.paris.fr
Closed Mondays

Rotating exhibits—the history of blue jeans, a review of haute couture, and so forth—may or may not include quilted needlework but are always of interest. Open during special exhibits only.

Musée Municipal de la Toile de Jouy
Château de l'Eglantine
54, rue Charles de Gaulle
Jouy-en-Josas (south of Paris near Versailles)
01 39 56 48 64
www.jouy-en-josas.fr (click on Decouvrir to find museum)
Closed Mondays

This museum holds a dazzling collection of *toiles de Jouy*, from the earliest eighteenth-century woodblock prints to scenic and allegorical toiles exhibited as they were used in costumes and quilted bed furnishings.

"Rags and tatters if you like: I am fond of my rags and tatters."

Molière, *L'avare* (*The Miser*) (1668)

Where to Buy French Quilts

For many collectors half the pleasure of acquiring treasures is the search, and finding a beautiful quilted bedcover from Provence can take some sleuthing. The American and British nineteenth-century hand-quilting traditions were more widespread than the French and consequently produced many more quilted textiles. When French pieces are found, they are likely to show their age and be expensive. Keep in mind the French appreciation for beauty at any age, in textiles as well as women.

When considering a purchase of a textile treasure, remember that Provence had a unique aesthetic in its quilting tradition that valued fanciful manipulation of surface texture. These four elements may be helpful in making an investment:

1. *Fabrics*. The French have manufactured a wealth of textile treasures for hundreds of years. Most printed cottons were made with long-staple cottons imported from India and Egypt; these are longer-wearing and more lustrous than short-staple cotton fabrics produced, for example, in the United States. Cotton prints dyed with natural dyes made from plant and mineral products have a richer color palette than those colored with the aniline dyes commonly used after about 1860. Older fabrics, especially if printed by woodblocks or copper plates, can be more valuable than those printed by copper rollers.

2. *Workmanship*. Eighteenth-century pieces are extremely rare but are truly wonderful acquisitions because of their exquisite needlework. However, some eighteenth-century pieces remain in Provence because their workmanship did not meet quality standards for export. Nineteenth-century quilts, produced for domestic consumption, were more crudely stitched but often reveal an attractive exuberance.

The aesthetic pleasure comes from the fabrics from which they were made and their quilting motifs, not the fineness of stitchery, a distinction that can be disconcerting to those who customarily hold high regard for miniature stitches. When trying to date a piece, remember that the sewing machine did not come into general use until about 1870.

3. *Design and proportion*. These two elements are critical in the composition of pleasing quilting motifs. Pieced work is not part of the Provençal tradition. However, a quilt having one fabric in the center and another in the border, the *fenêtre* composition, was commonly made in Provence. In nineteenth-century pieces quilting motifs should be worked in high, rounded relief, elegantly stitched if from the needle of a professional, more crude if done by a woman for her own use. Look for good proportion, pleasing color combinations in printed textiles, and interesting figures in the quilting.

4. *Condition*. Late-eighteenth-century and early-nineteenth-century fabrics can be fragile. Many dark brown colors printed on cotton were dyed with the addition of harsh mordants, which can corrode textile fibers. Mordant damage is difficult to repair because surrounding fibers have been weakened. Many silk fabrics were dipped in salts to make the fabric heavier and more lustrous; however, these salts may crystallize and cut silk fibers. Repair of damaged silk is nearly always futile. One should ask the seller how long any fabric has been exposed to air. If it has been open for a month and is still intact, no further deterioration, aside from abrasion, is likely to occur. If the piece has not been opened, oxidation may cause damage.

Antique French textiles bought for export should be accompanied by a bill of sale that includes the shop name, date of sale, description of item, the sales price, the seller's signature, and the estimated date of origin in numerals, for example "circa 1830." This last point is most important. The author has never been charged import duty on French textile items more than one hundred years old, but one U.S. Customs officer, presented with the phrase *"environs mille huit cents trente"* (circa 1830) on an invoice, asked how he was supposed to be able to read French and had to be convinced of the correct translation.

One last note: Antique textiles are more fragile than their modern counterparts. Request permission before handling a merchant's textile object, and handle it with care once permission is granted.

In Provence

Because Provence was the origin of French quilted needlework, there are several sources where they may be found. One occasionally happens on an old *couvre-lit* in a general antiques shop or at the seasonal antiques fairs, known as *foires des antiquaires* or *foires des brocantes* (check local newspapers for these). However, because most of these pieces are fairly ragged or more recent, it is more immediately rewarding to go to the few shops in Provence that specialize in antique textiles of all sorts. The following list includes some of the best sources in France.

Jérôme Beillieu
15, rue Gaston de Saporta
Aix-en-Provence
04 42 96 36 60 (call ahead)
www.textileantique.com

This new kid on the block has fabulous textiles.

F. Dervieux
5, rue Vernon
Arles
04 90 96 02 39
www.dervieux.com
Closed Sundays and holidays

This shop looks small on the outside but holds room on room of furniture and quilts, the latter easier to fit in one's suitcase. English spoken.

Foires des Brocantes et Antiquaires
c/o Office of Tourism
l'Isle-sur-la-Sorgue (near Avignon)
04 90 38 04 78

These fairs are definitely worth a visit for those with stamina and a good eye. They are held Easter and Assumption Day weekends. Verify dates with the office of tourism.

This town has several clusters of shops, open on weekends, where one occasionally can find a good Provençal quilt.

La Boutique de Francine
1, rue Julien Guigues
l'Isle-sur-la-Sorgue
04 90 38 55 81
Open weekends

Located in front of the railroad station, this shop is crammed to the beams with old textiles—in boxes, on shelves, peeking out of plastic sacks. Some English, lots of body language.

La Maison Biehn
7, avenue des Quatre Otages
l'Isle-sur-la-Sorgue
04 90 20 89 04
Open weekends and by appointment

No true passion for antique textiles can be requited without visiting La Maison Biehn, where some of the finest examples of eighteenth- and nineteenth-century needlework can be found and perfect English is spoken.

Nathalie Légier Antiquités
Avenue des Quatre Otages
l'Isle-sur-la-Sorgue
04 90 20 75 17
legier@antic-shop.com
Open weekends

A personable second-generation antiques dealer presents an array of quilted bedcovers amid stunning Provençal furniture.

Antiquités C. Fregosi
37, rue Falque
Marseilles
04 91 35 47 47 (call ahead)

It is hard to focus on the siren call of enticing textiles when so many decorative objects also clamor for attention.

Jean-Paul et Giselle Roche
Sausset-les-Pins (near Marseilles)
04 42 44 52 90 (call ahead)

Specialists in antique textiles from bedcovers to costume to wonderful collectors' morsels.

In Paris

Of the many possible sources of quilted textiles in Paris, the author has satisfactorily narrowed her regular shopping tours to the places listed below. There are many others, and readers are invited to explore. Despite the French interest in antiques, textiles and quilted textiles in particular remain a specialty item rarely available in a general antiques shop. Be sure to check Paris newspapers for announcements of neighborhood antiques fairs. Those passionate about doing quilting and patchwork themselves must go to Le Rouvray; the other listings are sources for antique textiles. Check weekly events periodicals, such as *Pariscope* and *L'Officiel,* for notice of auctions at Drouot called *ventes d'encheres* and for seasonal antiques fairs.

Le Rouvray
3, rue de la Bûcherie
01 43 25 00 45
www.lerouvray.com
Closed Sundays

Run by an American, this is the mecca for French quilting and patchwork enthusiasts. The shop is full of supplies and offers courses, including sessions in corded quilting.

Fanette
1, rue d'Alençon
01 42 22 21 73
Closed Sundays and Mondays

The selection of quilted works can be limited but is always satisfactory and shows the eye of a good dealer. Some English is spoken.

Marché aux Puces de Saint-Ouen
Several blocks from the Porte de Clignancourt
Métro stop
Open Saturdays, Sundays, and Mondays

This is the most famous (and overwhelmingly huge) flea market. Antique quilts may be found in several sections, although the most promising stalls are in the Marchés Serpette, Paul Bert, and Vernaison.

Village Saint-Paul
Off the rue Saint-Paul
01 48 87 91 02
Open days vary

This is another area of grouped shops where antique textiles may be found.

Glossary

The following French, Provençal, and English words and phrases relating to textiles are used throughout the book. Generally, a brief definition has been given on first mention in the text. More complete definitions are included here.

BÂTONS ROMPUS. A textile pattern showing small, articulated broken rods mingled with floral forms printed on cotton cloth.

BOURRETTE. A rough but long-wearing silk cloth woven from the outer fibers of the silkworm's cocoon.

BOUTIS. A Provençal word for the corded or quilted needlework used for petticoats, bedcovers, and infant lap pieces. Also, a blunt-nosed needle used to draw cording through narrow channels of stitching in *broderie de Marseille*.

BRODERIE DE MARSEILLE. Corded and stuffed needlework made in professional Marseilles ateliers during the seventeenth and eighteenth centuries. Two layers of fabric were stitched together along pattern lines, and then cording or stuffing was inserted into pattern channels and compartments to raise the surface relief.

CAMBRESINE. A finely woven cotton cloth imported from India and used to make *broderie de Marseille;* also known as *mousseline.*

CARACO. A short jacket with a fitted waist.

CHAFARCANIS. Small-scale, one- or two-color prints on coarsely woven white cotton, first imported from India and among the first to be imitated in Provençal print works.

CHAUFFOIR. A small quilted throw or an undergarment used to keep one warm.

COQUECIGRUE. Mythical Provençal creatures, encountered in woods and bushes, that tickle and bite, causing passersby to itch and squirm.

CORSET. An article of women's clothing, usually a type of fitted bodice, with or without sleeves.

COTILLON. A quilted petticoat worn as outerwear by Provençal women; also known as a *jupon* or *coutihoun.*

COTONINE. A weave combining cotton thread from India and hemp from Burgundy and produced only in Marseilles.

COURTEPOINTE. A quilted bedcover (literally, short stitches).

COUTIHOUN. The Provençal word for a quilted petticoat worn as outerwear by the women of Provence; also known as a *jupon* and *cotillon.*

COUVRE-LIT. A bedcover.

COUVRE-PIEDS. A small throw used to cover one's ankles, thereby preserving modesty, when reclining on a chaise longue.

ÉCAILLES IMBRIQUÉES. A textile pattern showing overlapped scales filled with small floral forms printed on cotton.

FENÊTRE. The composition of a Provençal bedcover made with a central textile with a border of a contrasting textile (literally, a window).

FICHU. A lightweight neck scarf.

GARNITURE. Bed furnishings—the curtains, upper and lower valances, canopy, and *courtepointe.*

HERBAGES. A textile pattern showing fields of small, bright flowers on a white or colored ground printed on cotton cloth.

INDIENNES. Painted or printed cotton cloth imported from India (hence the name) from the beginning of the seventeenth century. Motifs included flowers, mythic scenes, illustrated poems, and exotic scenes with flowering trees and wondrous animals. The first Provençal imitations were produced in Marseilles in 1648. In the nineteenth century the term *indiennes* was loosely applied to all printed cottons.

"ITALIAN QUILTING." Corded needlework identified with Sicily and Naples in the late fourteenth century; often inappropriately applied to *broderie de Marseille* produced in Provence.

JARDINIER. A textile pattern printed to the size of a *jupon* and showing multicolored, delicate arborescent trails in full bloom that extended from a luxuriant garden at the point of the *jupon's* hem.

JUPON. A quilted petticoat worn as outerwear by the women of Provence; also known as a *cotillon* or *coutihoun*.

KASHMIR CONES. Curved, tear-drop shapes often called paisley in English.

LINGE DU CORPS. Undergarments.

LISATS. White cotton weaves of fine quality from India used in making *broderie de Marseille* bedcovers.

"MARSEILLES CLOTH," "MARSEILLES QUILT." An ambiguous reference applied to an all-white cotton textile article with a raised, textured pattern, always whole cloth, in England and America since the eighteenth century. Before 1763 the pattern was created by handstitched needlework; after the invention of a loom that imitated handstitched work, the term referred to a loom-woven textile.

MATELASSÉ. A French word for quilted needlework of any technique, usually used in reference to a bedcover or an article of clothing.

MENUISER. A furniture maker.

MORDANTS. Metallic salts that are printed or painted on fabric and that adhere to the fibers, causing them to hold colors after immersion in a dying bath.

MOUSSELINE. A finely woven cotton cloth imported from India and used to make *broderie de Marseille;* also known as *cambresine*.

PETASSOUN. The Provençal word for a small infant lap piece used in the nineteenth century to protect the clothing of family members against accidents when holding a baby.

PILLEMENT PRINTS. Textile prints inspired by Chinese prints but incorporating fanciful flowers, exotic fruits, and fantasy parasols designed by Jean-Baptiste Pillement (1728–1808), court painter to Marie Antoinette. Pillement prints have appeared in furnishing prints ever since.

POINTE DE BEAUVAIS. Floral patterns embroidered on a base fabric in a chain stitch using silk or cotton thread.

QUILTING. The needlework technique of sandwiching a filling element, usually batting or cording, between two lengths of fabric, held together by lines of stitching.

RAMONEUR. A textile pattern showing multicolored flowers strewn on a dark brown field printed on cotton cloth.

TAPISSIER. An atelier that produced bed furnishings and other items for domestic decor.

TOILE. A textile.

TOILE BROCHÉE. Cotton, linen, or silk fabric on which floral patterns have been embroidered using colorful cotton, silk, or woolen thread.

TOILE DE JOUY. Printed fabric from the Oberkampf factory in Jouy-en-Josas near Paris, established in 1760.

TOILE PIQUÉE. Cloth worked with stitching. This term was used frequently in seventeenth-century France to refer to the quilted or corded work produced commercially in Marseilles.

VANHO. A Provençal word for *vanne*.

VANNE. The French word for a small quilted bedcover that rested on top of the bed for decorative effect; also known as *vanho*.

WHOLE CLOTH. Made of one type of fabric or weave, as in all-white, whole-cloth quilts; not pieced work except as seamed to make one large cover from different lengths of the fabric.

Further Reading

d'Agnel, Gustave Arnaud. *L'ameublement Provençal et Comtadin durant le moyen âge et la Renaissance*. Paris: 1926.

———. *Inventaires mobiliers du XIIIème siècle*. Vol. 1. Marseille: Tacussel, 1929.

Barthélemy, L. *Inventaire du château des Baux en 1426*. Paris: Imprimerie Nationale, 1878.

Beaumelle, Marie-José. "Les étoffes." In *Les arts décoratifs en Provence du XVIIe au XIXe siècle*. Aix-en-Provence: Edisud, 1993.

Beer, Alice Baldwin. *Trade Goods: A Study of Indian Chintz in the Collection of the Cooper-Hewitt Museum of Decorative Arts and Design, Smithsonian Institution*. Washington, D.C.: Smithsonian Institution Press, 1970.

Bertrand-Fabre, Danielle, and Robert Chamboredon. "Trousseau de mariée de Gabrielle Fornier, 1754." In *Les Fornier de Clausonne: Archives d'une famille de négociants de Nîmes (XVIIe–XIXe siècles)*. Nîmes: Archives Départementales du Gard, 1987.

Biehn, Michel. *En jupon piqué et robe d'indienne*. Marseille: Jeanne-Laffitte, 1987.

Blancard, Louis. *Documents inédits sur le commerce de Marseille au moyen âge*. Marseille: 1884.

Brédif, Josette. *Printed French Fabrics: Toiles de Jouy*. New York: Rizzoli, 1989.

Carfeuil, Gaspard. "Etat général de toutes les marchandises à Marseille en 1688." In *Encyclopédie méthodique: Commerce*. Vol. 2. Paris: Panckoucke, 1783.

Chabaud, Louis. *Marseille et ses industries: Les tissus, la filature et la teinturerie*. Marseille: La Société Scientifique-Industrielle de Marseille, 1883.

Clouzot, Henri. *Painted and Printed Fabrics: The History of the Manufactory at Jouy and Other Ateliers in France, 1760–1815*. New York: Metropolitan Museum of Art, 1927.

Colby, Averil. *Quilting*. New York: Charles Scribner's Sons, 1971.

Collier, Raymond, and Joseph Billioud. *Histoire du commerce de Marseille*. Vol. 3. Edited by Gaston Rambert. Paris: Chambre de Commerce de Marseille, 1951.

Cunnington, C. Willett. "Costume." In *The Late Georgian Period: 1760–1810*. Edited by Ralph Edwards and L.G.G. Ramsey. London: The Connoisseur, 1961.

Dow, George Francis. *Every Day Life in the Massachusetts Bay Colony*. Boston: Society for the Preservation of New England Antiquities, 1935.

Fukasawa, Katsumi. *Toilerie et commerce du Levant d'Alep à Marseille*. Paris: Editions du Centre National de la Recherche Scientifique, 1987.

Furetière, Antoine. *Dictionnaire universel*. The Hague and Rotterdam: Arnoul and Reinier Leers, 1690.

Garoutte, Sally. "Marseilles Quilts and Their Woven Offspring." In *Uncoverings, 1982*. Vol. 3. Mill Valley, Calif.: American Quilt Study Group, 1983.

Goubert, Pierre. *The Course of French History*. New York: Franklin Watts, 1988.

Grand Robert: Dictionnaire de la langue française. Paris: Dictionnaires le Robert, 1991.

Grosson, Georges. *Almanach historique de Marseille*. Marseille: 1771.

Hale, John. *The Civilization of Europe in the Renaissance*. New York: Simon and Schuster, 1993.

Harbeson, Georgiana Brown. *American Needlework*. New York: Bonanza Books, 1938.

Hersh, Tandy. "Eighteenth Century Quilted Silk Petticoats Worn in America." In *Uncoverings, 1984*. Vol. 5. Mill Valley, Calif.: American Quilt Study Group, 1985.

Holstein, Jonathan. "Sister Quilts from Sicily: A Pair of Renaissance Bedcovers." *The Quilt Journal* 3, no. 2 (1994): 14–15.

Intendance. Vols. 491 (1735) and 495 (1739). Archives Départementales des Bouches du Rhône, Marseille.

Janniere, Janine. "The 'Hand Quilting' of Marseille." *The Quilt Journal* 2, no. 1 (1993): 5–9.

Kohler, Carl. *A History of Costume.* New York: Dover Publications, 1963.

Lanier, Mildred B. "Marseilles Quiltings of the Eighteenth and Nineteenth Centuries." *Centre International d'Etude des Textiles Anciens Bulletin de Liaison,* nos. 47–48, I and II (1978): 74–82.

Lemire, Beverly. "Ready-made Clothing, Guilds, and Women Workers, 1650–1800." In *Dress.* Vol. 21. Earleville, Md.: Costume Society of America, 1994.

Levey, Santina M. "Embroidery." In *Textiles: 5,000 Years.* Edited by Jennifer Harris. New York: Harry N. Abrams, 1993.

Masson, Paul. *La Provence au XVIIIème siècle.* Paris: Librarie Hachette, 1936.

Mazet, J. Jh. *Guide Mazet.* Marseille: Firmin Isnard, 1789.

McClellan, Elisabeth. *Historic Dress in America: 1607–1800.* Philadelphia: George W. Jacobs and Company, 1904.

Mistral, Frédéric. *Calendau.* 1867. Reprint, Raphèle-lès-Arles: Marcel Petit, 1990.

——— . *Le Trésor du Félibrige.* 1886. Reprint, Raphèle-lès-Arles: Marcel Petit, 1968.

Montgomery, Florence. *Textiles in America: 1650–1870.* New York: W. W. Norton, 1984.

Pascal, Odile and Magali. *Histoire du costume d'Arles: Les formes sous l'Ancien Régime.* Paris: Octavo Editions, 1992.

The Quilters' Guild. *Quilt Treasures.* London: Deirdre McDonald Books, 1995.

Rambert, Gaston. *Histoire du commerce de Marseille, 1291–1480.* Vol. 2. Paris: Chambre de Commerce de Marseille, 1956.

——— . *Histoire du commerce de Marseille, 1660–1789.* Vol. 6. Paris: Chambre de Commerce de Marseille, 1959.

Rothstein, Natalie. *Silk Designs of the Eighteenth Century.* Boston: Bulfinch Press, 1990.

Roux, Annie. *Le textile en Provence.* Aix-en-Provence: Edisud, 1994.

Saint-Aubin, Charles Germain de. *L'art du brodeur.* Paris: 1770. See also Charles Germain de Saint-Aubin, *Art of the Embroiderer* [1770], translated by Nikki Scheuer and edited by Edward Maeder. Los Angeles: Los Angeles County Museum of Art and David R. Godine, 1983.

Sevigné, Madame de. *Selected Letters.* Translated by Leonard Tancock. New York: Penguin Books, 1982.

Suffolk County Probate Records, 1689–1703 (M-113, Inventories), Suffolk County, Mass. Inventory of Thomas Pemberton, November 30, 1693; Inventory of John Bankes, March 2, 1698; Inventory of Mrs. Jane Phelps, August 7, 1695. Joseph Downs Manuscript and Microfilm Collection, Winterthur Museum Library, Winterthur, Del.

Swan, Susan Burrows. *Plain and Fancy: American Women and Their Needlework, 1700–1850.* New York: Holt, Rinehart and Winston, 1977.

Teissier, Octave. *Meubles et costumes XVI–XVIII ème siècles.* Paris: Honoré Champion, 1904.

Verlet, Pierre. *La maison du XVIIIe siècle en France.* Paris: 1966.

Wainwright, Nicholas B. *Colonial Grandeur in Philadelphia.* Philadelphia: Historical Society of Philadelphia, 1964.

Acknowledgments

This book is the result of a long search for what I had thought must already exist—a book or museum collection that would be a font of information on the beautiful quilted needlework of Provence. That book did not exist until now and would not exist without all the wonderful friends and textile experts who encouraged my research with their generosity of ideas and information. From the beginning my curiosity was fanned by Jacqueline Jacqué, curator at the Musée de l'Impression sur Etoffes, Mulhouse, who generously invited me into the treasure trove of the museum's collection of textile documents in November 1990.

Most of the research for this book was done in France with the aid of many individuals who shared their wisdom and their collections, helped me gain access to numerous institutions, and tolerated my French, for which I am humbly grateful. My particular thanks go to Monique Alphand; Michel and Catherine Biehn; Evelyne Bremondy, curator of the Musée de Château-Gombert, Marseilles; Marie-Claude Desclozeaux; Thierry Guien; Monique Jay, librarian at the Musée des Tissus de Lyon; Madame Paul Ollivary and her daughter Catherine Gauthier; the costume historian Magali Pascal, and the photographer Bernard Touillon. I also thank Jean-Claude Gaudin, the mayor of the city of Marseilles, and Christian and Marie-José Beaumelle for making it possible to photograph at the Villa Provençale and the Villa Magalone.

For permission to photograph French quilts in their collections I thank Mesdames Alphand and Beaumelle; the Maison Biehn; Thierry Guien; Patricia Pepino, St. Tropez; and the Maison Quinta, Perpignan.

Jean-François Keller at the Musée de l'Impression sur Etoffes has my fervent gratitude for reviewing the text and correcting my errors.

My research in North America was aided by the following individuals, all of whom shared their knowledge and enthusiasm for this project with me: Linda Baumgarten, curator at Colonial Williamsburg; Helene Berger; Nancy Callaghan, *Country Living;* Claire Dimsdale; the late Sally Garoutte, whose 1982 article on French quilting launched my research; Edward Maeder, director of the Bata Shoe Museum in Toronto, Ontario; Joanie Pigford; Marjory Segal, needlework historian; Susan Burrows Swan; Nancy Tuckhorn, textile curator at the Daughters of the American Revolution Museum; and Fawn Valentine. To all them I express my grateful appreciation. I also thank Erik Kvalsvik for his beautiful photographs of this French needle art.

I am grateful to Diane Maddex, president of Archetype Press, for recognizing the importance of the Provençal needlework tradition and to Robert L. Wiser, designer, for presenting it so elegantly. My editor,

Gretchen Smith Mui, deserves high praise for her skills in clarifying information and smoothing rough syntax.

I am responsible for all translations from the French and errors I expect to be found in the text, for which I ask forbearance in advance.

Mary Wilson Balch, my mother, shared with me her brains and her passion for textiles. Robert Berenson embodied support, insight, and patience in the face of wild obsession. Elizabeth Dicker, my daughter, bore lengthy theory testing and innumerable heavy quilts with great spirit. To them, as the French say, big kisses!

The ten years since this book was first published have been splendid for the genre of French quilted needlework. The most stunning advance came in 2005, when the International Quilt Study Center at the University of Nebraska–Lincoln acquired my personal collection, one that has since been augmented by more wonderful pieces in preparation for the first North American exhibition of French quilted needlework in 2009. Bravo to Sara Dillow, Robert and Ardis James, and Carolyn Ducey.

Merci mille fois to Marie-Christine Flocard for her unflagging attention in the preparation of instructions for the projects in the third edition. Her experience and clarity of thinking are truly enabling. My thanks also go to our illustrator, Phoebe Adams Gaughan, who has beautifully rendered seven new projects.

I continue to thank those who originally helped me gather information in France for this book. They are Monique Alphand, Marie-José Beaumelle, Michel Biehn, Evelyne Bremondy, Marie-Claude Descloseaux, Catherine Gauthier, Thierry Guien, Jacqueline Jacqué, Monique Jay, Jean-François Keller, Magali Pascal, and Patricia Pepino. In the United States, my continuing thanks go to Linda Baumgarten, Helene Berger, *County Living,* Claire Dimsdale, Edward Maeder, Joanie Pigford, Susan Burrows Swan, Nancy Tuckhorn, and Fawn Valentine. Since the first publication, I have gained invaluable support from Anne-Rose Bringel, André-Jean Cabanel, and Bernard Jacqué.

Winterthur Museum also gets a bow for funding a study of their splendid French textile collection in the equally splendid company of its textile curator, Linda Eaton.

Much appreciation is also due Rosemary Ngo, Isa Loundon, and Celia Johnson of Potter Craft for their enthusiasm.

Always in my heart are four individuals who are no longer living but whose passion for these textiles illuminates this work: Byron M. Dillow, Sally Garoutte, Dédé Ollivary, and my mother, Mary Wilson Balch.

"Only connect!"
E. M. Forster, *Howards End* (1910)

Photograph Credits

Index